fastText Quick Start Guide

Get started with Facebook's library for text representation and classification

Joydeep Bhattacharjee

BIRMINGHAM - MUMBAI

fastText Quick Start Guide

Commissioning Editor: Sunith Shetty
Acquisition Editor: Reshma Raman
Content Development Editor: Aditi Gour
Technical Editor: Vaibhav Dwivedi
Copy Editor: Safis Editing
Project Coordinator: Hardik Bhinde
Proofreader: Safis Editing
Indexer: Tejal Daruwale Soni
Graphics: Jason Monteiro
Production Coordinator: Deepika Naik

First published: July 2018

Production reference: 1240718

Published by Packt Publishing Ltd.
Livery Place
35 Livery Street
Birmingham
B3 2PB, UK.

ISBN 978-1-78913-099-7

www.packtpub.com

"To my wife, Saionee, for patiently hearing my ideas and giving me advice, support, and motivation, to get this book done, and to my mom, father-in-law, and mother-in-law for their love and support."

- Joydeep Bhattacharjee

mapt.io

Mapt is an online digital library that gives you full access to over 5,000 books and videos, as well as industry leading tools to help you plan your personal development and advance your career. For more information, please visit our website.

Why subscribe?

- Spend less time learning and more time coding with practical eBooks and Videos from over 4,000 industry professionals

- Improve your learning with Skill Plans built especially for you

- Get a free eBook or video every month

- Mapt is fully searchable

- Copy and paste, print, and bookmark content

PacktPub.com

Did you know that Packt offers eBook versions of every book published, with PDF and ePub files available? You can upgrade to the eBook version at www.PacktPub.com and as a print book customer, you are entitled to a discount on the eBook copy. Get in touch with us at service@packtpub.com for more details.

At www.PacktPub.com, you can also read a collection of free technical articles, sign up for a range of free newsletters, and receive exclusive discounts and offers on Packt books and eBooks.

Contributors

About the author

Joydeep Bhattacharjee is a Principal Engineer who works for Nineleaps Technology Solutions. After graduating from National Institute of Technology at Silchar, he started working in the software industry, where he stumbled upon Python. Through Python, he stumbled upon machine learning. Now he primarily develops intelligent systems that can parse and process data to solve challenging problems at work. He believes in sharing knowledge and loves mentoring in machine learning. He also maintains a machine learning blog on Medium.

I'd like to thank to Sherin Thomas for help on PyTorch, and Deepayan Das and Kalyan Ram for their help on the Android sections.

Thanks to the Packt team for believing in me, to Reshma Raman for pushing me on the initial drafts, Aditi Gour for the helpful advice, reviews, and for coordinating the whole process, and Vaibhav Dwivedi for the final technical reviews and bringing the book to publishing.

About the reviewer

Krishna Modi is Managing Director at CodeAngle Technologies Pvt. Ltd.

Before starting his company, he worked with enterprises like Cisco Systems and Hewlett Packard Enterprises as a Consultant. He was also an SME for Cloud and Infrastructure Management at Fork Media Pvt. Ltd. Krishna has interest in Data Science and System Programming. He is a registered teaching faculty with ICAI and has been a speaker at various national and international technical sessions hosted by ICAI.

Krishna enjoys writing for technical magazines like PC Quest, Open Source For You and has contributed multiple articles on technology updates for AskMen India Edition.

> *I have to start by thanking my parents, getting in depth knowledge about the topic would not be possible without their constant support and encouragement. Special thanks to the superwoman in my life, Roshni, my beloved wife. She was as important to this book getting done as I was.*
> *Thanks to everyone on the publishing team for choosing me for this task.*
> *Thank you readers for making this a success.*

Packt is searching for authors like you

If you're interested in becoming an author for Packt, please visit `authors.packtpub.com` and apply today. We have worked with thousands of developers and tech professionals, just like you, to help them share their insight with the global tech community. You can make a general application, apply for a specific hot topic that we are recruiting an author for, or submit your own idea.

Table of Contents

Preface

FastText is a state-of-the-art tool that can be used to perform text classification and build efficient word representations. It is open source and is designed at **Facebook Artificial Intelligence Research** (**FAIR**) lab. It is written in C++, and you also have wrappers available in Python.

This book has the ambitious goal of covering all and techniques and know-how that you need to build NLP applications in the real world. It will also cover the algorithms on which fastText is built so that you will clearly understand the context in which you can expect the best results from fastText.

Who this book is for

This book will be of benefit to you if you are a software developer/machine learning engineer trying to understand the state-of-the-art in NLP. A large part of the book deals with real-life problems and considerations for creating an NLP pipeline. If you are an NLP researcher, there is a lot of value here because you will learn about the internal algorithms and considerations taken while developing the fastText software. All the code examples are written in Jupyter Notebooks. I highly recommend you type them out, change them, and tinker with them. Keep the code handy so that you can use it later in your actual projects.

What this book covers

Chapter 1, *Introducing FastText*, introduces fastText and the NLP context in which this library is useful. It will map the motivations behind building the library and the intended usage and benefits that the creators of the library intended to bring into NLP and the field of computational linguistics. There will also be specific instructions explaining how to install fastText on your work machine. Upon completion of this chapter, you will have fastText installed and running on your computer.

Chapter 2, *Creating Models Using the FastText Command Line*, discusses the rich command line that the fastText library provides. This chapter describes the default command-line options and shows how to use it to create models. If you are only interested in having a superficial introduction to fastText, reading up to this chapter should be enough.

`Chapter 3`, *Word Representations in FastText*, explains how unsupervised word embeddings are created in fastText.

`Chapter 4`, *Sentence Classification in FastText*, introduces the algorithms that power sentence classification in fastText. You will also learn how fastText compresses big models into smaller models that can be deployed to low-memory devices.

`Chapter 5`, *FastText in Python*, is about creating models in Python by either using the official Python bindings for fastText or by using the gensim library, which is a popular Python library for NLP.

`Chapter 6`, *Machine Learning and Deep Learning Models*, explains how to integrate fastText into your NLP pipeline if you have pre-built pipelines that use either statistical machine learning paradigms or deep learning paradigms. In the case of statistical machine learning, this chapter makes use of the scikit-learn library; and in the case of deep learning, Keras, TensorFlow, and PyTorch are taken into account.

`Chapter 7`, *Deploying Models to Mobile and the Web*, is mainly about deployment and how to integrate fastText models in live production-grade customer applications.

To get the most out of this book

Ideally, you should have a basic knowledge of how Python code is written and structured. If you are not familiar with Python or are not clear how programming languages work in general, then please take at look at a book on Python. A book dealing with Python from a data science perspective would be ideal for you.

If you already have a basic idea of NLP and machine learning in general, this book should be easy for you to grasp. If you are starting out in NLP, that should not be too much of an issue if you are willing to dive deep into the mathematics covered. I have taken care to explain the mathematical concepts covered in this book, but if this too seems too difficult, please write to us and let us know.

A willingness on the part of the reader to dive deep and try out all the code is assumed.

Download the example code files

You can download the example code files for this book from your account at `www.packtpub.com`. If you purchased this book elsewhere, you can visit `www.packtpub.com/support` and register to have the files emailed directly to you.

You can download the code files by following these steps:

1. Log in or register at `www.packtpub.com`.
2. Select the **SUPPORT** tab.
3. Click on **Code Downloads & Errata**.
4. Enter the name of the book in the **Search** box and follow the onscreen instructions.

Once the file is downloaded, please make sure that you unzip or extract the folder using the latest version of:

- WinRAR/7-Zip for Windows
- Zipeg/iZip/UnRarX for Mac
- 7-Zip/PeaZip for Linux

The code bundle for the book is also hosted on GitHub at `https://github.com/PacktPublishing/fastText-Quick-Start-Guide`. In case there's an update to the code, it will be updated on the existing GitHub repository.

We also have other code bundles from our rich catalog of books and videos available at `https://github.com/PacktPublishing/`. Check them out!

Conventions used

There are a number of text conventions used throughout this book.

`CodeInText`: Indicates code words in text, database table names, folder names, filenames, file extensions, pathnames, dummy URLs, user input, and Twitter handles. Here is an example: "Commands such as `cat`, `grep`, `sed`, and `awk` are quite old and their behavior is well-documented on the internet."

A block of code is set as follows:

```
import csv
import sys
w = csv.writer(sys.stdout)
for row in csv.DictReader(sys.stdin):
 w.writerow([row['stars'], row['text'].replace('\n', '')])
```

When we wish to draw your attention to a particular part of a code block, the relevant lines or items are set in bold:

```
import csv
import sys
w = csv.writer(sys.stdout)
for row in csv.DictReader(sys.stdin):
    w.writerow([row['stars'], row['text'].replace('\n', '')])
```

Any command-line input or output is written as follows:

```
$ cat data/yelp/yelp_review.csv | \
  python parse_yelp_dataset.py \
 > data/yelp/yelp_review.v1.csv
```

Bold: Indicates a new term, an important word, or words that you see on screen. For example, words in menus or dialog boxes appear in the text like this. Here is an example: "Select **System info** from the **Administration** panel."

Warnings or important notes appear like this.

Tips and tricks appear like this.

Get in touch

Feedback from our readers is always welcome.

General feedback: Email feedback@packtpub.com and mention the book title in the subject of your message. If you have questions about any aspect of this book, please email us at questions@packtpub.com.

Errata: Although we have taken every care to ensure the accuracy of our content, mistakes do happen. If you have found a mistake in this book, we would be grateful if you would report this to us. Please visit www.packtpub.com/submit-errata, selecting your book, clicking on the Errata Submission Form link, and entering the details.

Piracy: If you come across any illegal copies of our works in any form on the Internet, we would be grateful if you would provide us with the location address or website name. Please contact us at copyright@packtpub.com with a link to the material.

If you are interested in becoming an author: If there is a topic that you have expertise in and you are interested in either writing or contributing to a book, please visit authors.packtpub.com.

Reviews

Please leave a review. Once you have read and used this book, why not leave a review on the site that you purchased it from? Potential readers can then see and use your unbiased opinion to make purchase decisions, we at Packt can understand what you think about our products, and our authors can see your feedback on their book. Thank you!

For more information about Packt, please visit packtpub.com.

1
First Steps

On completion of this section, the reader will have working knowledge of how to install fastText and run the command line application effectively on any dataset.

In the Chapter 1, *Introducing fastText*, you will get a description of fastText and the Natural Language Processing (NLP) context in which this library is useful. It will map the motivations behind building the library, its intended use, and the benefits that the creators of the library wanted to bring to NLP and the field of Computational Linguistics. Furthermore, there will be specific instructions on how to install fastText on the reader's work machine. On completion of this chapter, the reader will have fastText installed and running on their computer.

In the Chapter 2, *Creating Models Using the FastText Command Line*, you will get to know about the rich command line that the fastText library provides. This chapter will give you descriptions of the default command line options and how to use them to create models. If the reader only has a superficial interest in fastText, reading till this chapter should be enough.

1
Introducing FastText

Welcome to *fastText Quick Start Guide*. In this first chapter, you will find out how to install fastText and create a stable environment in which to learn how to use fastText applications as part of your Natural Language Processing applications.

fastText is a library that helps you to generate efficient word representations and gives you support for text classification out of the box. In this book, we will take a look at a specific use case, namely machine translation, and use fastText for that. We have chosen machine translation because fastText claims that it is superior in terms of yet unknown words, and can handle different languages for which sufficiently large data sources and corpora may not be available. In different chapters, we will see how fastText fares in such cases. General techniques will also be discussed so that you will be able to extend those techniques to your specific use case. We will cover the following topics in this chapter:

- Introducing fastText
- Installing fastText in Windows, Linux, and macOS
- Using a Docker image for fastText
- Installing dependencies on Mac systems
- Installing Python dependencies
- Installing dependencies on RHEL machines using the yum package manager
- Installing dependencies on Debian-based machines such as Ubuntu
- Installing dependencies on Arch Linux using pacman

Introducing fastText

In today's interconnected world, a lot of text data gets generated around the world. This text information includes descriptions of things. Take, for example, people writing about products in Amazon reviews, or people writing about their thoughts through their Facebook posts. **Natural Language Processing** (**NLP**) is the application of machine learning and other computational techniques to understanding and representating spoken and written text. The following are the major challenges that NLP seeks to solve:

- **Topic modeling**: In general, texts deal with a topic. Topic modeling is frequently used to determine hidden structures or "abstract topics" that may be present in a collection of documents. An effective application of topic modeling would be summarization. For example, legal documents are quite complex and verbose, and hence systems such as these would help the reader to get the gist of the document and a high-level description of what is happening.

- **Sentence classification**: Text classification is a important challenge, where we are able to take in blobs of text and classify them into different labels. For example, a system should be able to correctly classify something like "Shahrukh Khan was on fire at Dubai event" as belonging to the label "Entertainment" and another sentence, "Fire breaks out in store opposite Breach Candy Hospital," to be categorized as "News."

- **Machine translation**: The total number of languages in the world is at least 3,000. About half of these languages have fewer than 10,000 speakers and about 25 percent have less than 1,000 speakers. Hence, we can imagine that a lot of languages are dying and when a language dies, collectively we lose a lot of our cultural heritage. The best translation system right now is made by Google, but it covers only 103 languages at the time of writing, so it is very important that we develop machine learning translation models that are able to train from few sources with a high degree of predictive power.

- **Question and answer (QA) systems**: The focus here is to build a system that automatically answers questions based on the questions that people ask in natural language. QA systems that can be built around closed domain systems can be highly accurate as they can retrieve documents and text that are relevant to the search item.

- **Sentiment analysis**: Sentiment analysis is about understanding the needs and intents that the users share when talking about something. People make choices based on emotions. The needs of many people are largely emotional and, generally, people are very forthcoming about how they feel. Creating a system that takes this into account will always add a lot of value to the business.
- **Event extraction**: Use cases involve where a lot of data is stored in the form of text. For example, some legal text may be describing a "crime" event, which is followed by an "investigation" event, which is followed by multiple "hearing" events. The events themselves may be nested such that the "hearing" events may consist of a "presenting arguments" events and a "presenting evidence" events.
- **Named entity detection**: The focus of building this system is to extract and classify entities or specific information as per some predefined categories, such as people, organization, geography, and so on. For example, if we take the following text: "We're used to spicy foods down here in South Texas," we can understand that the "buyer" likes "spicy foods" and his "geography" is South Texas. If there is sufficient evidence received from the data that buyers in South Texas like spicy foods, more such foods can be marketed to them.
- **Relation detection**: A relation detection system parses text and identifies focal points and agents, then tries to find the relationship between them. For example, the sentence "Mike has the flu" can be converted to `Person-[RELATION:HAS]->Disease`. These relations can then be explored in a business context to build intelligent apps.

The previous list has many of the problems that NLP practitioners are targeting. Depending on the use case, you can pick up any of these challenges and try to solve them in your domain. The challenge with many previous approaches and modeling techniques is that NLP requires a lot of textual data and there is a lot of contextual information in the data. It is quite hard for a computational model to get a sense of all the data in an efficient manner. NLP models up to now have only targeted English as textual data is available in English. But only 20 percent of the population of the world speak English and even among them, the majority are non-native speakers. The biggest deterrent to building non-English NLP models is the lack of data. Hence, we desperately need libraries that can build models even when the data is limited. fastText has the potential to change all that. The fastText team has published pretrained word vectors for 294 languages. By the time the book is published, more languages will have been added to it.

In this chapter, we will see how to install fastText so that you can start tinkering with this amazing software.

Some of the descriptions provided may not be applicable to you; for example, instructions for Mac users may not be directly relevant to Linux users and vice versa. Still, I would suggest that you read through the whole description for each of the dependencies for a better understanding.

Installing fastText

Depending on your operating system, you will need to make sure that you have some dependencies installed in your machine. In this section, you will get to know how to install fastText based on whether you are using a Linux, Windows, or macOS operating system. Additionally, you will get to know what additional dependencies you should install depending on your usage. My recommendation is to install all the software packages, as we will be exploring all the various ways we can use fastText in this book.

Prerequisites

FastText works on Windows, Linux, and macOS. FastText is built using the C++ language, so you will first need a good C++ compiler.

Windows

Official binaries for Windows are not available, but you can download the latest Windows binaries compiled by Meng Xuan Xia at the following link: `https://github.com/xiamx/fastText/releases`. To run these binaries, you will need to install Visual C++ 2017. You can download the 64-bit versions of Visual C++ from this link: `https://support.microsoft.com/en-in/help/2977003/the-latest-supported-visual-c-downloads`. Next, the usual way of installing, by double-clicking on the installer file for Visual C++, should install it on your Windows machine.

Linux

The list of prerequisite software that you need to install is as follows:

- GCC-C++; if you are using Clang, you will need 3.3 or newer
- Cmake
- Python 3.5 (you can work with Python 2.7, but we are going to focus on Python 3 in this book)

- NumPy and SciPy
- pybind

Optional requirements, depending on your system, are as follows:

- Zip
- Docker
- Git

Installing dependencies on RHEL machines supporting the yum package manager

On Linux machines, you will need to have g++ installed. On Fedora/CentOS, which supports the yum package manager, you can install g++ using the following command. Open the Terminal or connect to the server where you are installing this using your favorite SSH tool and run the following command:

```
$ sudo yum install gcc-c++
```

CMake should be installed by default. The official docs have the installation instructions in make and cmake. I would recommend installing cmake on your machine and using it to build fastText. You can directly install cmake using the yum generic command like before:

```
$ sudo yum install cmake
```

To get a full list of cmake commands, take a look at the following link: https://cmake.org/cmake/help/v3.2/manual/cmake.1.html.

To install the optional software, run the following command:

```
$ sudo yum install zip docker git-core
```

If you are starting on a new server and running yum commands there, then you may encounter the following warning:

```
Failed to set locale, defaulting to C
```

In this case, install the glibc language pack:

```
$ sudo yum install glibc-langpack-en
```

Now, you can jump to the installation instructions for Anaconda to install the Python dependencies.

Installing dependencies on Debian-based machines such as Ubuntu

In Ubuntu and Debian machines, `apt-get` or `apt` is your package manager. `apt` is basically a wrapper around `apt-get` and other similar tools, and hence you should be able to use them interchangeably. I will be showing `apt` commands here but if you are using older versions of Ubuntu and Debian, and see that apt is not working on your machines, then you can replace `apt` with `apt-get` and it should work. Also, consider upgrading your machine if possible.

Similar to Fedora, to install C++, open a Terminal or SSH into the server where you are going to install fastText and run the following command. This will also install the `cmake` command:

```
$ sudo apt update
$ sudo apt install build-essential
```

Now install `cmake`:

```
$ sudo apt install cmake
```

To install the optional requirements, run the following command:

```
$ sudo apt install zip docker git-core
```

Now, check the Anaconda section to see how to install Anaconda for the Python dependencies.

 The `apt` command only works from Ubuntu-16 onwards. If you are using an older Ubuntu version, you should use the `apt-get` command.

Installing dependencies on Arch Linux using pacman

The package manager of choice on Arch Linux is pacman and you can run the following command to install the essential build tools:

```
$ sudo pacman -S cmake make gcc-multilib
```

This should install the make, cmake, and g++ compiler that you need to build fastText. Although Arch distributions already have Python 3.x installed, I would recommend installing Anaconda as described later in this chapter so that you don't miss out on any of the Python dependencies.

To install the optional requirements, run the following command:

```
$ sudo pacman -S p7zip git docker
```

Installing dependencies on Mac systems

On macOS, you should have Clang installed by default, which is designed to be a drop-in replacement for the normal compilers for C, C++, and other similar languages. Check whether the version is 3.3 or later using clang --version in a Terminal. If you do not have Clang or something from the older versions, then you can install using the xcode command-line tools using a Terminal:

```
$ xcode-select --install
```

A dialog should appear next that asks if you want to install the developer tools. Click on the **Install** button.

Installing Python dependencies

I recommend that you install Anaconda so that there are no issues with installing Python and using it for fastText. Detailed instructions for installing Anaconda are given on the official documentation page, which can be accessed at https://conda.io/docs/user-guide/install/linux.html. Simply stated, if you are on Windows, then download the Windows installer, double-click on it, and then follow the instructions on the screen. Installing it using a GUI is also possible for macOS.

In the case of Linux and macOS, download the corresponding bash file and then run the following command in a Terminal:

```
$ bash downloadedfile.sh
```

Please take care to download and install it using installers that are tagged for Python 3.x. The Python code snippets that will be shown in this book will be shown for Python 3.x.

Installing fastText on Windows

Currently, official binaries are not provided for fastText on Windows, and hence there is no GUI to install fastText on your machine. To use fastText, you will need to perform the following steps:

1. Download the latest binary named **fasttext-win64-latest-Release.zip** from the release page provided by Xua (https://github.com/xiamx/fastText/releases).
2. This is a ZIP file and hence you will need to extract the contents. You will find the fasttext_pic.lib, fasttext.lib, fasttext.exe, and fasttext.dll files in the extracted folder. This folder will be your working directory for fastText:

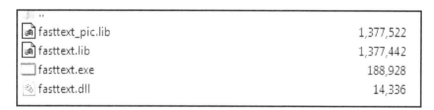

3. Create a folder, data where you will keep all your data files. Now, open PowerShell and change directory to the folder.
4. Type .\fasttext.exe in Powershell and you should be able to see the output.

If you don't see any output at the end, then you probably don't have Visual C++ Redistributable in your machine and will need to install that.

Installing fastText in Linux and macOS

To install fastText, run the following commands to clone the image and build it in a Terminal:

```
$ git clone https://github.com/facebookresearch/fastText.git
$ cd fastText
$ mkdir build && cd build && cmake ..
$ make && make install
```

In this book, a lot of focus will be on building systems for Python. So, run the following commands as well in the same directory:

```
$ pip install .
```

`pip` is the package manager for Python. fastText assumes UTF-8 encoded text, which is the default in Python 3.x. The Python code examples in this book will be shown using Python 3.x. One of the advantages of fastText is that you can build fastText models for multiple languages and if you are not using Python 3.x, then you will not be able to take advantage of this. If that is not a concern and you are trying to use fastText using Python 2.7, then take a look at the *Appendix* at the end, which will give you guidelines on how to develop, keeping in mind UTF-8 in Python 2.7.

Using a Docker image for fastText

You can also use Docker to run fastText on your machine and not worry about building it. This can be done to maintain version control between specific versions and thus gives us predictability and consistency. You can get information on how to install Docker from the following link: `https://docs.docker.com/install/#cloud`.

After installing, start the Docker service before running the following commands:

```
start the docker service.
$ systemctl start docker

# run the below commands to start the fasttext container.
$ docker pull xebxeb/fasttext-docker
```

You should now be able to run fastText:

```
$ mkdir -p /tmp/data && mkdir -p /tmp/result
$ docker run --rm -v /tmp/data:/data -v /tmp/result:/result \
        -it xebxeb/fasttext-docker ./classification-example.sh
```

You may need to provide permissions and create the specific directories to run the `docker run` command.

Summary

In this chapter, you have taken a look at how to install and start using fastText in the environment of your choice.

In the next chapter, we will be taking a look at how to train fastText models using the command line and how to use them.

2
Creating Models Using FastText Command Line

FastText has a powerful command line. In fact, you can call fastText a command-line-first library. Now, a lot of developers and researchers are not comfortable with the command line, and I would ask you to go through the examples in this chapter with greater attention. My hope is that by the end of this chapter, you will have some confidence in command-line file manipulations. The advantages of using the command line are as follows:

- Commands such as `cat`, `grep`, `sed`, and `awk` are quite old and their behavior is well-documented on the internet. Chances are high that, for any use case that you might have, you will easily get snippets on Stack Overflow/Google (or your colleague next door will know it).
- Since they are generally implemented in the C language, they are very fast.
- The commands are very crisp and concise, which means there is not a lot of code to write and maintain.

We will take a look at how classification and word vector generation works in fastText. In this chapter, we will explore how to implement them using the command line:

- Text classification using fastText
- FastText word vectors
- Creating word vectors
- Facebook word vectors
- Using pretrained word vectors

Text classification using fastText

To access the command line, open the Terminal on your Linux or macOS machines, or the command prompt (by typing cmd in Windows + *R* and hitting *Enter*) on Windows machines, and then type fastText. You should see some output coming out. If you are not seeing anything, or getting an error saying that the command not found, please take a look at the previous chapter on how to install fastText on your computer. If you are able to see some output, the output is a basic description of all the options. A description of the command line options for fastText can be found in the *Appendix* of this book.

 All the methods and command line statements mentioned in this chapter will work on Linux and Mac machines. If you are a Windows user, focus more on the description and the logic of what is being done and follow the logic of the steps. A helpful guide on command line differences between Windows and Linux is mentioned in the *Appendix*.

In fastText, there are two primary use cases for the command line. These are the following:

- Text classification
- Text representation

One of the core areas of focus for fastText is text classification. Text classification is a technique in which we learn to which set of categories the input text belongs. This is basically a supervised machine learning problem, so first and foremost, you will need a dataset that contains text and the corresponding labels.

Roughly speaking, machine learning algorithms run some kind of optimization problem on a set of matrices and vectors. They do not really understand "raw text," which means that you will need to set up a pipeline to convert the raw text into numbers. Here are the steps that can be followed to do that:

- First, you need the data and hence for text classification you need a series of texts or documents that will be labeled. You convert them into a series of text-label pairs.
- The next step is called **tokenization**. Tokenization is the process of dividing the text into individual pieces or tokens. Tokenization is primarily done by understanding the word boundaries in the given text. Many languages in the world are space delimited. Examples of these are English and French. In some other cases, the word boundaries may not be clear, such as in the case of Mandarin, Tamil, and Urdu.

- Once the tokenization is done, based on the process you may end up with a "bag of words," which is essentially a vector for the document/sentence telling you whether a specific word is there or not, and how many times. The columns in the matrix are all the set of words present, which is called the dictionary, and the rows are the count of the particular words in the document. This is called the **bag-of-words** approach.
- Convert the bag of words into a TF-IDF matrix to reduce the weight of the common terms. TF-IDF has been used so that the terms that are common in the document do not have too much impact on the resultant matrix.
- Now that you have the matrix, you can pass the matrix as input to a classification algorithm, which will essentially *train a model* on this input matrix. General algorithms that are quite popular in this stage are logistic regression, as well as algorithms such as XGBoost, random forest, and so on.

Some of the additional steps that may need to be taken are the following:

- Removal of stop words.
- Stemming or a heurestic removal of end of words. This process works mostly in English and related languages due to the prevalence of derivational affixes.
- Addition of n-grams to the model.
- Synonymous sets.
- Part of speech tagging.

Text preprocessing

Depending on the dataset, you may need to do some or all of these steps:

- Tokenize the text.
- Convert the text into lowercase. This is only required for languages using Latin, Greek, Cyrillic, and Armenian scripts. Examples of such languages are English, French, German, and so on.
- Strip empty lines and their correspondences.
- Remove lines with XML tags (starting with <).

These steps should be done in both cases, for sentence classification as well as the creation of word vectors.

English text and text using other Roman alphabets

We will understand text processing using a sample dataset. In this chapter, the Yelp dataset is used. This is a popular dataset containing text reviews and the ratings given by users. In this dataset, you will find information about businesses in 11 metropolitan areas in four countries. If you download the data from the Kaggle link where it is shared, https://www. kaggle.com/yelp-dataset/yelp-dataset/data, there are various files we will see, but in our case we will only be interested in the review text provided by users in the yelp_review.csv file. As a challenge, we will try to see whether we can correctly predict the ratings or not.

Downloading the data

Since this information is related to a particular business, and in case you are interested in downloading and playing with the data, please take a look at these steps before downloading the data:

1. Please review the Yelp dataset webpage.
2. Please review, agree to, and respect Yelp's terms of use.
3. Download yelp_review.csv from Kaggle. The link for that is here: https://www.kaggle.com/yelp-dataset/yelp-dataset/data.

This is the code:

```
$ mkdir -p data/yelp
$ cd data/yelp
$ mv ~/Downloads/yelp_review.csv.zip .
$ unzip yelp_review.csv.zip
Archive: yelp_review.csv.zip
  inflating: yelp_review.csv
```

Preprocessing the Yelp data

Take a look at the data. Always take a deep look at the data. The first line contains the headers:

```
$ head -n1 yelp_review.csv
"review_id","user_id","business_id","stars","date","text","useful","funny",
"cool"
```

When you check the other lines, you will see that all the individual values are quotes. Also, the text field has new lines in many places. Since the strength of fastText is in text processing, we will only be taking the "stars" and the "text" fields, and will try to predict the ratings based on what is written in the text field.

You can use the following Python script to save the text and the ratings to another file, since the review text has a lot of new lines and we needed to remove the new lines from the text. You can keep them if you want and change the new line to another delimiter so that the file is fastText-compatible, but for our example we will remove the new lines from the text.

Here is the Python code to get only the relevant parts of the .csv:

```
import csv
import sys
w = csv.writer(sys.stdout)
for row in csv.DictReader(sys.stdin):
    w.writerow([row['stars'], row['text'].replace('\n', '')])
```

Save this in a file named parse_yelp_dataset.py and then run the following command:

```
$ cat data/yelp/yelp_review.csv | \
 python parse_yelp_dataset.py \
 > data/yelp/yelp_review.v1.csv
```

Text normalization

In this section, will take a look at some text normalization techniques that you can use.

Removing stop words

The removal of stop words may or may not increase the performance of your model. So, keep two files, one with the stop words and one with the stop words stripped out. We will talk about how to check model performance in the *Model testing and evaluation* section.

You can use the following script to remove the stop words. This is a Python script with dependencies such as nltk, so use it with your Anaconda installation. Please ensure that you have already downloaded the nltk 'english' package before running the following script:

```
$ python -c "import nltk; nltk.download('stopwords')"
```

Save the following code in a file named `remove_stop_words.py`:

```python
import io
from nltk.corpus import stopwords
from nltk.tokenize import word_tokenize
import sys
def get_lines():
    lines = sys.stdin.readlines()
    for line in lines:
        yield line
stop_words = set(stopwords.words('english'))
for line in get_lines():
    words = line.lower().split()
    newwords = [w for w in words if w not in stop_words]
    print(' '.join(newwords))
```

To run the file, you will need to pass the contents to the Python file. In the following explanations though, we are not really removing the stop words for the sake of brevity. You are of course encouraged to try both approaches.

Normalizing

Since we are dealing with English, it is recommended to first convert all uppercase letters to lowercase as follows:

```
$ cat data/yelp/yelp_review.v1.csv \
    | tr '[:upper:]' '[:lower:]' \
    > data/yelp/yelp_review.v2.csv
```

Languages using the Latin, Greek, Cyrillic, and Armenian scripts are bicameral, which means that there are uppercase and lowercase letters. Examples of these are English, French, and German. Only in such languages should you be careful to convert all the text to lowercase. While processing a corpus for other languages, this step is not required.

Now, the start of the files already has all the labels. If we prefix the start of all sentences with __label__, it will add all the labels with the __label__ text. This prefixing of the labels is necessary as the library takes in the whole text as the input, and there is no specific way to specify the input and the labels separately, as you might have seen in `scikit-learn` or other libraries. You can change the specific label prefix though, as you will see in the *Appendix*.

So, to read the file in fastText and enable fastText to differentiate between normal text and label text, you will need to append __label__ to the labels. One of the ways you can do that easily in the command line is shown here:

```
$  cat data/yelp/yelp_review.v2.csv \
    | sed -e 's/^/__label__/g' \
    > data/yelp/yelp_review.v3.csv
```

Separate out and remove some of the punctuation that may be irrelevant:

```
$ cat data/yelp/yelp_review.v3.csv \
    | sed -e "s/'/ ' /g" \
    -e 's/"//g' -e 's/\./ \. /g' -e 's/<br \/>/ /g' \
    -e 's/,/ , /g' -e 's/(/ ( /g' -e 's/)/ ) /g' \
    -e 's/\!/ \! /g' \
    -e 's/\?/ \? /g' -e 's/\;/ /g' \
    -e 's/\:/ /g' > data/yelp/yelp_review.v4.csv
```

Do not forget to keep checking how the data has been transformed after each transformation. On checking the data now, you can see that there is a comma at the beginning. There are also a lot of dots (.):

```
$ head -n 2 data/yelp/yelp_review.v4.csv
  __label__5 , super simple place but amazing nonetheless . it ' s been
around since the 30 ' s and they still serve the same thing they started
with a bologna and salami sandwich with mustard . staff was very helpful
and friendly .
  __label__5 , small unassuming place that changes their menu every so often
. cool decor and vibe inside their 30 seat restaurant . call for a
reservation . we had their beef tartar and pork belly to start and a salmon
dish and lamb meal for mains . everything was incredible ! i could go on at
length about how all the listed ingredients really make their dishes
amazing but honestly you just need to go . a bit outside of downtown
montreal but take the metro out and it ' s less than a 10 minute walk from
the station .
```

Remove the commas and the dots. Keep in mind that fastText does not require the removal of punctuation and lowercasing all the letters; in fact, in some cases these may be important. Remember to take all the advice given here with a grain of salt and try all possible options you can think of. The ultimate aim is to train the best model.

```
cat data/yelp/yelp_review.v4.csv | sed 's/\,//g' >
data/yelp/yelp_review.v5.csv
cat data/yelp/yelp_review.v5.csv | sed 's/\.//g' >
data/yelp/yelp_review.v6.csv
mv data/yelp/yelp_review.v6.csv data/yelp/yelp_review.v5.csv
```

Finally, remove all the consecutive spaces. Please note that in the following example, after all these transformations, the files are no longer in the `.csv` format, but that is fine for us because at the end of the day, `.csv` files are also text files and hence you should be fine with using `.txt` or any other textual format. As long as the files are text files with the contents in UTF-8 format, you should be good to go.

```
$ cat data/yelp/yelp_review.v5.csv | tr -s " " >
data/yelp/yelp_review.v6.csv
```

Shuffling all the data

Shuffling the data before training the classifier is important. If the labels for the data are clustered, then the precision and recall, and hence the performance of the resulting model, will be low. This is because fastText uses stochastic gradient descent to learn the model. The training data from the files is processed in order. In our example, this is not the case as the labels of the same class are not together, but still it may be a good idea to keep this in mind and always shuffle before training.

In *Nix systems, you have the shuffle command, as follows:

```
$ cat data/yelp/yelp_review.v6.csv | shuf > data/yelp/yelp_review.v7.csv
```

Sometimes, the shuffle command is quite slow and you may want to consider using the `perl` one-liner in the case of large files:

```
$ perl -MList::Util -e 'print List::Util::shuffle <>' \
    data/yelp/yelp_review.v6.csv \
    > data/yelp/yelp_review.v8.csv
```

Dividing into training and validation

Model performance evaluation should always be done on independent data. You should always separate out your whole dataset into train and test sets. But, dividing too much also reduces the amount of data that you have for training, so 80% is a good midpoint. You can divide the file into an 80-20 split using the following command:

```
$ awk -v lines=$(wc -l < data/yelp/yelp_review.v9.csv) \
    -v fact=0.80 \
    'NR <= lines * fact {print > "train.txt"; next} {print > "val.txt"}' \
    data/yelp/yelp_review.v9.csv
```

Model building

In this section, we take a look at how to go about the steps of model training and evaluation.

Model training

Now, you can start the training step:

```
$ fasttext supervised -input data/yelp/train.txt -output
result/yelp/star_model
```

The output will be shown when training, and at the end you should get an output similar to this:

```
Read 563M words
 Number of words: 1459620
 Number of labels: 5
 Progress: 100.0% words/sec/thread: 3327124 lr: 0.000000 loss: 0.789366
ETA: 0h 0m
```

If you now check the `result/yelp/` directory, you should be able to see two files with extensions `.vec` and `.bin`. The `.bin` file is the trained classifier. The `.vec` file has all the words with the vectors for the individual words. You can open the `.vec` file. It is just a text file. However, take care to open it using a lightweight text editor such as Sublime Text or Notepad++, as it will be a big file. Or, just use command line tools such as `head` or `tail`.

Here are some of the vectors created in our case. The first line has the dimensions of the vectors, which are (`1459620, 100`) in our case. The next two lines are the vectors for `.` and the:

```
1459620 100
 . -0.080999 ... -0.029536
 the -0.022696 ... 0.084717
```

Model testing and evaluation

Now that you know how to create model files in fastText, you will need to test and check the performance of your model, and report its efficacy in real terms. This can be done using various performance measures.

Precision and recall

To test the accuracy of a classification model, two parameters that are very popular and are supported by fastText are precision and recall. Recall is the percentage of labels that are correctly recalled of all the labels that actually exist, and precision is the percentage of all the labels that were predicted correctly. These two parameter values can be checked using the following command:

```
$ fasttext test result/yelp/star_model.bin data/yelp/val.txt
 Now     1052334
 P@1     0.685
 R@1     0.685
 Number of examples: 1052334
```

The precision and recall are currently at 68%. Let's optimize some parameters and see if we can make the model better.

Confusion matrix

Now that you have a model, you can also see the performance of the model with respect to the different labels using the confusion matrix. Along with precision and recall, confusion matrices give a good idea of the **true negatives** (**TN**) and the **false positives** (**FP**) as well. In an ideal world, all the diagonals have high values, while all the remaining cells have negligible values, but in a real scenario, you may need to chose if you are OK with having high FP values or high **false negative** (**FN**) values.

To get the confusion matrix, you will need to do some post-processing. Separate the sentences from the labels. Then, using the predict command, you will be able to predict the label for each test line. A Python script is provided, which can be used to get the confusion matrix:

```
$ mv data/yelp/val.testlabel data/yelp/val.testsentences
$ cut -f 1 -d ' ' data/yelp/val.txt > data/yelp/val.testlabel
$ cut -f 2- -d ' ' data/yelp/val.txt > data/yelp/val.testsentences
$ fasttext predict result/yelp/star_model.bin data/yelp/val.testsentences >
pexp
$ python fasttext_confusion_matrix.py data/yelp/val.testlabel pexp
 Accuracy: 0.716503505541
 [[124224 16161 3347 864 1639]
 [ 24537 39460 19435 2748 1283]
 [ 5514 15646 63775 32668 5424]
 [ 1445 1815 22583 139956 78795]
 [ 1707 548 3071 59103 386586]]
```

You can download the Python script from this gist: `https://gist.github.com/loretoparisi/41b918add11893d761d0ec12a3a4e1aa#file-fasttext_confusion_matrix-py`. Or, you can get it from the GitHub repository:

```
import argparse
import numpy as np
from sklearn.metrics import confusion_matrix
def parse_labels(path):
    with open(path, 'r') as f:
        return np.array(list(map(lambda x: x[9:], f.read().split())))
if __name__ == "__main__":
    parser = argparse.ArgumentParser(description='Display confusion
matrix.')
    parser.add_argument('test', help='Path to test labels')
    parser.add_argument('predict', help='Path to predictions')
    args = parser.parse_args()
    test_labels = parse_labels(args.test)
    pred_labels = parse_labels(args.predict)
    eq = test_labels == pred_labels
    print("Accuracy: " + str(eq.sum() / len(test_labels)))
    print(confusion_matrix(test_labels, pred_labels))
```

Hyperparameters

There are multiple hyperparameters that can be supplied when training the model to improve the model. Take a look at some of the hyperparameters here and their effects on model training.

Epoch

By default, fastText takes a look at each data point five times. You can change this using the `-epoch` command. In the following example, we change the epoch parameter to 25 and see whether there is any improvement in our model:

```
$ fasttext supervised -input data/yelp/train.txt -output
result/yelp/star_model -epoch 25
 Read 563M words
 Number of words:  1459620
 Number of labels: 5
 Progress: 100.0% words/sec/thread: 3451048 lr: 0.000000 loss: 0.761496
ETA: 0h 0m
```

The result of the model is 68.6% for precision and recall, which is only a 0.1% improvement:

```
P@1 0.686
R@1 0.686
```

Learning rate

This may be because we already have a huge number of samples. Another important hyperparameter that we can change is the learning rate, using the $-lr$ argument. The learning rate controls how "fast" the model updates during training. This parameter controls the size of the update that is applied to the parameters of the models. Changing the learning rate from 0.025 to 1.0 means that the updates that are applied to the model are 40 times larger. In our model, we could also see that the learning rate was becoming 0 at the end. This means that the model was not learning at all by the end. Lets try to make the learning rate as 1 and see what happens:

```
$ fasttext supervised -input data/yelp/train.txt -output
result/yelp/star_model -lr 1.0
 Read 563M words
 Number of words: 1459620
 Number of labels: 5
 Progress: 100.0% words/sec/thread: 3381014 lr: 0.000000 loss: 0.847610
ETA: 0h 0m
```

The result for this model was the same as before. There was no difference when changing the learning rate:

```
P@1 0.686
R@1 0.686
```

N-grams

We have one more hyperparameter that may have a huge influence on the performance of the model. By default, when creating word vectors for the model, unigrams are used. Unigrams are n-grams where n is 1. N-grams can be best explained using the following diagram:

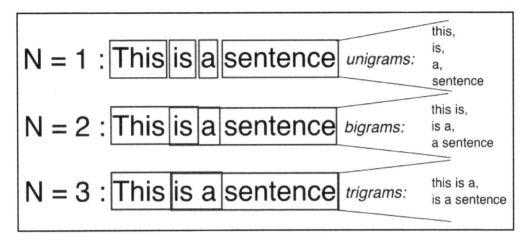

Source: https://stackoverflow.com/a/45477420/5417164

You also can fix the value of N in fastText using the -wordNgrams parameter:

```
$ fasttext supervised -input data/yelp/train.txt -output
result/yelp/star_model -wordNgrams 2
 Read 563M words
 Number of words: 1459620
 Number of labels: 5
 Progress: 100.0% words/sec/thread: 1141636 lr: 0.000000 loss: 0.687991
ETA: 0h 0m
```

Now, the precision and recall are 71.8%, which is a 3.2% improvement. Lets try for some more:

```
$ fasttext supervised -input data/yelp/train.txt -output
result/yelp/star_model -wordNgrams 3
 Read 563M words
 Number of words: 1459620
 Number of labels: 5
 Progress: 100.0% words/sec/thread: 620672 lr: 0.000000 loss: 0.633638 ETA:
0h 0m
 $ fasttext test result/yelp/star_model.bin data/yelp/val.txt
 Now1052334
 P@1    0.717
 R@1    0.717
 Number of examples: 1052334
```

Making N = 3 resulted in a decrease in performance. So, let's keep the value of N as 2.

You can combine all the parameters to create the new model:

```
$ fasttext supervised -input data/yelp/train.txt -output
result/yelp/star_model -wordNgrams 2 -lr 1.0 -epoch 10
```

Start with pretrained word vectors

If the text corpus that you have is not huge, it is generally advised to start with some pretrained word vectors for the language that you are training the classifier for, or the classification results may be poor. How to create word vectors from your corpus is handled in depth in the next section.

```
$ fasttext supervised -input data/yelp/train.txt -output
result/yelp/star_model_withprevecs -pretrainedVectors wiki-news-300d-1M.vec
-dim 300
 Read 563M words
 Number of words: 1459620
 Number of labels: 5
 Progress: 100.0% words/sec/thread: 1959282 lr: 0.000000 loss: 0.788021
ETA: 0h 0m
```

In our case, there was not much improvement. The precision and recall increased marginally and stood at 68.5%.

Finding the best fastText hyperparameters

FastText has a lot of hyperparameters that you can optimize to find the right balance for your model. For a classifier, you can start with the loss functions, see whether changing the character n-grams makes sense, and see whether changing the learning rate and dimensions have any effect.

A popular algorithm for implementing hyperparameter optimization is using the grid-search approach. Since your aim is to find a good model, you will have a training dataset and a test dataset. Let's say the training data is the `train.txt` file and the test data is the `test.txt` file. You are essentially solving an optimization problem (P), which is the function of the combination of weights in this case w and the hyperparameters, be in n-grams, learning rate or epochs.

So, you understand that solving the optimization problem for a fixed set of values for the hyperparameters gives you a specific model. Since the optimal model (call it model*) is a function of the hyperparameters, we can write it as follows:

$$model^*(ngrams, learningrate, epochs) = P(model, ngrams, learningrate, epochs, training_data)$$

Now, you can use this model* to predict on the training data to get the accuracy. Thus, the goal of hyperparameter optimization is to find the set of hyperparameters that gives the highest accuracy.

Note that this calculation of the best model is going to be quite expensive. There is no magic mantra, no magic formula to find the hyperparameters for the best model. Just taking one hyperparameter, the learning rate, would make the calculation impractical. This is a continuous variable and you would need to feed in each specific value, compute the model, and check the performance.

Therefore, we resort to a grid search: basically, picking a bunch of values for the hyperparameters based on a heurestic, and based on all the combinations of the values, feeding them into the calculation and picking the set of values with the best performance.

This is called a grid search because the set of values that are considered, when plotted on a graph, look like a grid.

How you can implement this is by defining an array of values for your hyperparameters:

```
dim=(10 20)
lr=(0.1 0.3)
epochs=(5 10)
```

Now, we have a global variable where we will save the individual variables, as and when we find better models, and initialize them to be 0. We will also have a global performance variable to store the present best performance and set it to 0 initially. In this case, since we are experimenting with three hyperparameters, we will have the variable as length 3, as you can see here:

```
final=(0 0 0)
performance=0
```

Now comes the implementation of the `for` loops that will cycle through all the combinations of the values. Note that the depth of the `for` loop would be based on the number of hyperparameters that you are cycling through:

```
for z in ${dim[@]}
do
    for y in ${lr[@]}
    do
        for x in ${epochs[@]}
        do
            # train with the current set of parameters
            ...
            # test the current model
            ...
```

```
                        # see if current model is the best model and update the final
    variable.
                    ...
        done
    done
done
```

As you can probably guess, since we are checking for two values each for the three hyperparameters, the number of times training will happen is 2 x 2 x 2 = 8. So, if each training step takes, say, 5 minutes, that would mean that the total process will take 8 x 5 minutes or 40 minutes.

Now, let's go to the mean. Here is the training step:

```
$ ./fasttext supervised -input train.txt -output model -dim "$z" -lr "$y" -epoch "$x"
```

Once the training is done, then comes the test phase. We save the test data to a file so that we can compare the results later:

```
$ ./fasttext test model.bin test.txt > performance.txt
```

Now comes the comparison and saving the best models:

```
present_performance=$(cat performance.txt | awk 'NR==2 {print $2}') # get
the precision values
if (( $(echo "$present_performance > $performance" | bc -l) )); then
    # if current performance is the best performance till date
    final[0]="$z"
    final[1]="$y"
    final[2]="$x"
    echo "Performance values changed to ${final[@]}"
    echo "present accuracy:"
    cat performance.txt
fi
```

Now, you can extend this script to bring in more hyperparameters as well. You can find the whole code in the repo in the file.

Model quantization

With the help of model quantization, the fastest models have the ability to fit on mobile and on small devices such as Raspberry Pi. Since the code is open source, there are Java and Swift libraries that can be used to load the quantized models and serve them in Android and iOS apps respectively.

The algorithm for compressing the fastText models was created with collaboration between fastText and the **Facebook AI Research** (**FAIR**) team. This results in the reduction of fastText models by a huge amount. FastText models that are of the range of hundreds of MB get reduced to around 1-2 MB.

Implementing quantization can be done using the quantize argument. You will need to train a model with the normal route though:

```
$ DATADIR=data
$ RESULTDIR=result
$ ./fasttext supervised -input "${DATADIR}/train.txt" -output
"${RESULTDIR}/model" -dim 10 -lr 0.1 -wordNgrams 2 -minCount 1 -bucket
10000000 -epoch 5 -thread 4
Read 298M words
Number of words: 1454893
Number of labels: 5
Progress: 100.0% words/sec/thread: 2992746 lr: 0.000000 loss: 0.634722 eta:
0h0m
$ fastText-0.1.0 git:(master) ./fasttext quantize -output
"${RESULTDIR}/model" -input "${DATADIR}/train.txt" -qnorm -retrain -epoch 1
-cutoff 100000
Progress: 100.0% words/sec/thread: 2382426 lr: 0.000000 loss: 0.711356 eta:
0h0m h-14m
```

Note that there is a huge difference between the quantized model and the unquantized one:

```
$ du -sh $RESULTDIR/model.bin
466M result/yelp/model.bin
$ du -sh $RESULTDIR/model.ftz
1.6M result/yelp/model.ftz
```

The .bin file is about 466 MB, while the quantized model is just 1.6 MB.

Interestingly there seems to be a slight increase in precision and recall values.

```
$ ./fasttext test $RESULTDIR/model.bin $DATADIR/val.txt
N 1052334
P@1 0.699
R@1 0.699
Number of examples: 1052334
$ ./fasttext test $RESULTDIR/model.ftz $DATADIR/val.txt
N 1052334
P@1 0.7
R@1 0.7
Number of examples: 1052334
```

So you get almost no difference in performance and a good saving in space. You can now deploy this model in a smaller device. In the next chapter, we will discuss how this model quantization works. Also, in `Chapter 7`, *Deploying Models to Web and Mobile*, we will discuss how you can package a quantized model as part of an Android app.

Unfortunately, quantization only works for supervised models for now, but this may change in the future, so keep your fastText installation updated.

Understanding the model

Once the model is created, you can now see the parameters that were used while generating the model. This can be useful later when you are thinking deeper about your data and would like to change some model parameters, or for general documentation purposes:

```
$ fasttext dump result/yelp/star_model.bin args
  dim 100
  ws 5
  epoch 5
  minCount 1
  neg 5
  wordNgrams 2
  loss softmax
  model sup
  bucket 2000000
  minn 0
  maxn 0
  lrUpdateRate 100
  t 0.0001
```

The `dict` parameter gives information on the dictionary of words that was used in training. In the preceding training procedure, 1,459,625 words have been used, which can be seen as follows. `was` is used 8,272,495 times, `crinkle-also` is used only once in the whole set of sentences, and so on. It also gives information on whether the word is used as a word or a label. As you can see, the labels are listed at the end:

```
$ fasttext dump result/yelp/star_model.bin dict > dumpdict
$ ls -lhrt dumpdict
 -rw-rw-r-- 1 joydeep joydeep 27M Apr 2 11:05 dumpdict
$ head dumpdict
 1459625
 . 34285218 word
 the 23539464 word
 , 16399539 word
```

```
and 16299051 word
i 14330427 word
a 12034982 word
to 11508988
' 8907643 word
was 8272495 word
$ tail dumpdict
m&m\/chocolate 1 word
drops-surprisingly 1 word
crinkle-also 1 word
cookie-humungo 1 word
dishes\/restaurants 1 word
__label__5 1802332 label
__label__4 978722 label
__label__1 585128 label
__label__3 492454 label
__label__2 350698 label
```

The rows of the dump of input and output correspond to the parameters of the model. In our model, the first 1,459,620 rows of input are the vectors associated to the individual words, while the remaining 2 million rows are used to represent subwords. Those 2 million subwords were chosen to represent the overall meaning and can be understood from the bucket parameter in the output for the dump of the args as well. The rows of output are the vectors associated to the context or our labels. Usually, when learning unsupervised word representations, these are not kept after training:

```
$ fasttext dump result/yelp/star_model.bin input > dumpinput
$ cat dumpinput | wc -l
3459621
$ fasttext dump result/yelp/star_model.bin output > dumpoutput
$ cat dumpoutput | wc -l
5
```

The transformations mentioned in this section can be seen in the transformations.sh file in the GitHub repository.

FastText word vectors

The second major focus of fastText is creating word embeddings for the input text. During training, fastText looks at the supplied text corpus and forms a high-dimensional vector space model, where it tries to encapsulate as much meaning as possible. The aim of creating the vectors space is that the vectors of similar words should be near to each other. In fastText, these word vectors are then saved in two files, similar to what you have seen in text classification: a .bin file and a .vec file.

In this section, we will look at the creation and use of word vectors using the fastText command line.

Creating word vectors

We will now take a look at how to go about creating word vectors in fastText. You will probably be working with and building a solution for a specific domain, and in such a case, my advice would be to generate the raw text from the specific domain. But in cases where the raw text is not available to you, then you can use the help of Wikipedia, which is a huge collection of raw text in multiple languages.

Downloading from Wikipedia

To start with word vectors, you will need data or a text corpus. If you are lucky, you have the text corpus available to you. If you are not so lucky, which you will eventually be if you are interested in solving interesting problems in NLP, you will not have the data with you. In those cases, Wikipedia is your friend. The best thing about Wikipedia is that it is the best source of written text in more than 250 languages from around the world. Granted that is a minuscule number compared to the number of languages there are, but still that will probably be enough for most of your use cases. And if you are working in a language for which there are not enough Wikipedia resources, maybe you should raise awareness of how important Wikipedia is in your language community and ask the community to contribute to Wikipedia more. Once you know your target language, you can download the Wikipedia corpus using the `get-wikimedia.sh` file. You can get this file from the GitHub repository of fastText. A slightly updated version of the file can be copied from the *Appendix*.

Use the `get-wikimedia.sh` file to download the Wikipedia corpus.

You can get the list of all the languages that Wikipedia has articles on at this link: `https://meta.wikimedia.org/wiki/List_of_Wikipedias`. At this link, the list of languages is given in this format:

№ ◆	Language ◆	Language (local) ◆	Wiki ◆	Articles ◆
1	English	English⊕	en	5,603,394⊕
2	Cebuano	Sinugboanong Binisaya⊕	ceb	5,383,028⊕
3	Swedish	Svenska⊕	sv	3,783,784⊕
4	German	Deutsch⊕	de	2,169,391⊕
5	French	Français⊕	fr	1,971,039⊕
6	Dutch	Nederlands⊕	nl	1,927,858⊕

It is the third column that needs your attention. Note down the third value for your language of choice and run `bash get-wikimedia.sh`:

```
$ bash get-wikimedia.sh
 Saving data in data/wikimedia/20180402
 Choose a language (e.g. en, bh, fr, etc.): ja
 Chosen language: ja
 Continue to download (WARNING: This might be big and can take a long
time!)(y/n)? y
 Starting download...
 --2018-04-02 19:32:40--
https://dumps.wikimedia.org/jawiki/latest/jawiki-latest-pages-articles.xml.
bz2
 Resolving dumps.wikimedia.org (dumps.wikimedia.org)... 208.80.154.11,
2620:0:861:1:208:80:154:11
 Connecting to dumps.wikimedia.org
(dumps.wikimedia.org)|208.80.154.11|:443... connected.
 HTTP request sent, awaiting response... 200 OK
 Length: 2656121742 (2.5G) [application/octet-stream]
 Saving to: 'data/wikimedia/20180402/jawiki-latest-pages-articles.xml.bz2'

 jawiki-latest-pages-articles.xml.bz 0%[
```

You will receive a BZ2 file. To uncompress a BZ2 file, run the following command:

```
bzip2 -d enwiki-20170820-pages-articles.xml.bz2
```

If you open the file (be careful while doing this, the file is huge), you will find a lot of unnecessary stuff, such as HTML tags and links. So, you will need to clean the text with the `wikifil.pl` script, which was written by Matt Mahoney. This script is distributed with the fastText GitHub files.

Text normalization

If you have downloaded the English corpus, you can use the `wikifil.pl` script:

```
perl wikifil.pl data/enwik9 > data/fil9
```

In our case, we have the Japanese text and hence we will be using WikiExtractor (`https://github.com/attardi/wikiextractor`) to extract the text from the BZ2 file:

```
find data/jap_wiki/cleaned_jap_text.txt/ -type f -exec cat {} \; | python
japanese_parser.py -d /var/lib/mecab/dic/ipadic-utf8 >
data/jap_wiki_parsed.txt
```

There are still a lot of tags and English words that are part of the tags. You will need to do some more processing and text cleaning to make the corpus ready for training:

```
$ cat data/jap_wiki_parsed.txt | sed "s/^.*https.*$//g" >
  data/jap_wiki_parsed1.txt
 $ cat data/jap_wiki_parsed1.txt | tr '[:upper:]' '[:lower:]' >
data/jap_wiki_parsed2.txt
 $ cat data/jap_wiki_parsed2.txt | sed
  "s/[abcdefghijklmnopqrstuvwxyz]//g" > data/jap_wiki_parsed3.txt
 $ cat data/jap_wiki_parsed3.txt | tr -s " " >
  data/jap_wiki_parsed4.txt
 $ cat data/jap_wiki_parsed4.txt | awk 'NF' | awk '{$1=$1;print}' >
  data/jap_wiki_parsed5.txt
```

Now, you can go ahead and start the training process. We will keep the English numbers.

Create word vectors

Now, you can create the word vectors. Create the `result` directory:

```
$ mkdir -p result/jap_wiki
  fasttext skipgram -input data/jap_wiki_parsed5.txt -output
  result/jap_wiki/jap
```

There are two algorithms that are supported by fastText for creating word vectors, `skipgram` and `cbow`:

```
$ fasttext skipgram -input data/jap_wiki/fil_cleaned_jap_text3.txt -
  output result/jap_wiki/jap
```

and

```
$ fasttext cbow -input data/jap_wiki/fil_cleaned_jap_text3.txt -output
  result/jap_wiki/jap_cbow
```

Model evaluation

Model evaluation for word vectors is largely a manual process. In such cases, you can try some samples of the words and see if the model gives adequate results.

Some of the methods that you can use for model evaluation are looking at the nearest neighbors of the model and looking at some word analogies. One popular method is through t-SNE visualizations. We will look at t-SNE visualizations in `Chapter 4, Sentence Classification in FastText`.

Nearest neighbors

To get the nearest neighbors of a given word, pass the `nn` argument, and then you will need to give the path to the BIN file. For brevity, we will show only three results here:

```
$ fasttext nn result/jap_wiki/jap.bin
 Pre-computing word vectors... done.
 Query word? 眠る
本土復帰  0.949732
ハチノス  0.945276
国政選挙  0.943492
```

Similar words to sleep (眠る) give the previous results, which mean "return to the mainland"; "Hachinosu," which is a peak in Antarctica; and "national election." The results are random in our case and therefore not good.

Word analogies

Word analogies are a good way of finding out whether the model is working or not. How analogies work is that two groups of words with similar relationships should be separated by similar distances in the vector space. So, when you provide words for man, woman, and king, the result should be queen, as in a good vector space, the distance between word vector denoting "man" and the word vector denoting "woman" should be close to the distance between the word vector denoting "king" and the word vector denoting "queen." The command shows 10, but here only the top three are shown:

```
$ fasttext analogies result/jap_wiki/jap.bin
  Query triplet (A - B + C)? おとこ 女性 キング   (man woman king)
 *クラッキング  0.856853
 モンキーキング  0.855393
 *キング  0.852085
```

The meaning of the symbols in this code block are "cracking," "Monkey King," and "King", which are not very helpful in our case.

Other parameters when training

Similar to supervised learning, you can change various hyperparameters and see whether the models that are created work better. So, you can fix the minimal number of word occurrences with the `-minCount` parameter and the maximum length of word n-grams with the `-wordNgrams` parameter. You can change the number of buckets that fastText uses to hash the word and character n-grams to limit memory use. If you have a huge memory in your system, you can change this bucket parameter by passing a larger value than 2 million to see whether your model performance increases using the `-bucket` parameter. You can change the minimum and maximum length of character n-grams using the parameters `-minn` and `-maxn`. Change the sampling threshold using `-t`, change the learning rate using `-lr`, change the rate of updates for the learning rate using `-lrUpdateRate`, change the dimensions of the word vectors using `-dim`, change the size of the context window using `-ws`, change the number of epochs, which is the number of times each row is looked at during training, from the default 5 using `-epoch`, change the number of negatives sampled using `-neg`, and change the loss function that is used from the default **ns (negative sampling)** to softmax or **hs (hierarchical softmax)**. The default number of threads used is 12, but generally people have four cores or eight cores, and hence you can change the number of threads to optimally use the cores using the `-thread` parameter.

Out of vocabulary words

FastText also supports out of vocabulary words. FastText is able to do that because it not only keeps track of word-level N-grams, but also character-level n-grams. So, things like "learn," "learns," and "learned" look similar to it. To get the vectors for out of vocabulary words, you have to use binary models, which means the model files with the `.bin` extension:

```
$ fasttext print-word-vectors wiki.it.300.bin < oov_words.txt
```

Facebook word vectors

Facebook has released a large number of pretrained word vectors based on Wikipedia and common crawling, which you can download from their website and use in your projects (`https://fasttext.cc/docs/en/pretrained-vectors.html`). The common crawl models are CBOW models, and the wiki models are skip-gram models. Vectors are of dimensions 300 and character n-grams of length 5 are used, and a window size of 5 and 10 negatives are used.

Using pretrained word vectors

You can use pretrained word vectors for your supervised learning task. This has been discussed briefly under supervised learning. An example command is shown as follows:

```
$ fasttext supervised -input train.txt -output model -epoch 25 -
  wordNgrams 2 -dim 300 -loss hs -thread 7 -minCount 1 -lr 1.0 -verbose
  2 -pretrainedVectors wiki.ru.vec
```

There are some things that need to be taken care of while using pretrained vectors. You can find them at `https://stackoverflow.com/questions/47692906/fasttext-using-pre-trained-word-vector-for-text-classification`.

Machine translation

Facebook has done a lot of work on neural machine translation in the form of MUSE. MUSE is a library for multilingual unsupervised and supervised word embeddings. MUSE uses and is built on top of fastText word embeddings. The word embeddings that you get with fastText are monolingual, and hence the vectors need to be aligned to effectively translate from one language to the other. As part of MUSE, see the following features:

- fastText Wikipedia supervised word embeddings for 30 languages were released. These word embeddings are aligned in a single vector space.
- 110 large-scale ground truth bilingual dictionaries were also released so that you can train your own models.

Summary

In this chapter, you took a look at how you can combine the command line text transformation capabilities of the *Nix shell and the fastText library to implement a training, validation, and prediction pipeline. The commands that you explored in this chapter are not only versatile, they are fast as well. Having good mastery over the command line, along with a fastText app, should enable you to create fast prototypes and deploy them in a fast-paced environment. With this, the first part of the book is complete.

The next part of the book is about the theory and algorithms that have gone into making the package, with the next chapter being about unsupervised learning using fastText.

The FastText Model

2

On completion of this section, you will have working knowledge of how fastText goes about creating both supervised and unsupervised models. Additionally, you will have knowledge of the algorithms and the design decisions that went into incorporating those algorithms into fastText.

In the Chapter 3, *Word Representations in FastText*, you will get to know how unsupervised word embeddings are created in fastText.

In the Chapter 4, *Sentence Classification in FastText*, you will get to know about the algorithms that power sentence classification in fastText. You will also get to know how fastText is able to compress big models into smaller models that can be deployed to low memory devices.

The aim of this section is to shine a light on the algorithms and design choices in fastText, and give you the knowledge to generate better models or augment the library.

3
Word Representations in FastText

Now that you have taken a look at creating models in the command line, you might be wondering how fastText creates those word representations. In this chapter, you will get to know what happens behind the scenes and the algorithms that power fastText.

We will cover the following topics in this chapter:

- Word-to-vector representations
- Types of word representations
- Getting vector representations from text
- Model architecture in fastText
- The unsupervised model
- fastText skipgram implementation
- **CBOW** (**Continuous bag of words**)
- Comparison between skipgram and CBOW
- Loss functions and optimizations
- Softmax
- Context definitions

Word-to-vector representations

Almost all machine learning and deep learning algorithms manipulate vectors and matrices. The reason they work is because of their base mathematics, which is heavily rooted in linear algebra. So, in short, for both supervised and unsupervised learning, you will need to create matrices of numbers. In other domains, this is not an issue as information is generally captured as numbers. For example, in retail, the sales information for how many units were sold or how much revenue the store is making in the current month is all numbers. Even in a more abstract field such as computer vision, the image is always stored as pixel intensity of the three basic colors: red, green, and blue. 0 for a particular color means no intensity and 255 means the highest possible intensity for the screen. Similarly, in the case of sound, it is stored as power spectral density coefficients. In the case of sound, the analog signal that is picked up by the microphone is then converted to a discrete time and discrete amplitude. The amplitude is essentially the number of bits that can be passed in a given amount of time and hence that is essentially a number.

The challenge that comes in raw text in computer systems is that they are stored and analyzed as strings, which do not work well with these matrix systems. So you need a method to convert text into matrices.

Types of word representations

Depending on the target languages, there are various concepts that should be taken care of for an optimal word representation of the given corpus:

- **Distributed word representation**: In a distributed representation, the sense of the word should not be concentrated on only one dimension but be distributed across all dimensions. If it is not distributed, then the resulting vectors may be too big, which can be a limiting factor when performing the necessary vector transformations both in terms of memory and the time needed to perform the transformations. A distributed representation is compact and can represent an exponential number of clusters in the number of dimensions.
- **Distributional word representation**: You can argue that there is some kind of similarity between "cat" and "dog" and another kind of similarity between "cat" and "tiger". Word representations that focus on capturing those kinds of implicit relationships are called distributional. To get such distributional properties, the following very common paradigm is used:

You shall know the meaning of the word by the company it keeps

- John Rupert Firth (1962)

So if we take an example with two sentences, "Mary has a cat" and "Mary has a dog", the context around "dog" and "cat" is the same and hence the word representation should be able to get the "pet" context by reading the two sentences.

- **Zipf's law and Heap's law**: We will have some more discussion on Zipf's law when we go to the n-grams but we will state Heap's law here:

The number of distinct words in a document (or set of documents) as a function of the document length (so called type-token relation).

Taken together, Heap's law and Zipf's law are essentially saying the same thing, which is that you will always have new words. Hence, you should not be throwing away rare words from the document and will need a word representation that is more welcoming of new words. You cannot model language, close the vocabulary, and say you are done.

Getting vector representations from text

In this section, we will take a look at what it means to have a vector representation for the target group of text. We will start with one of the simplest forms of word vectors and how to implement it. Then we will explore the rationale behind some other types of word vectors and, finally, we will take an in-depth look at the algorithms that are used in fastText to create the word vectors.

One-hot encoding

In the simplest approach, raw text can be taken as a collection of tokens, where are assumption is that each "word" contributes in some way to the meaning of the sentence as a whole. All words are meant to signify something specific and hence are categories by themselves. The presence of a word would mean the presence of the category for which the word stands for, and absence of the word would mean that the category is not there. Hence, the traditional method was to represent categorical variables as binary variables. First the dictionary of words is created and then each word is assigned a unique position. Then the vectors are created by putting 1 in the respective index and 0 for all other variables. This system of creating vectors is called one-hot encoding:

```
['eat']      ->      [ 0.  1.  0.]
['sleep']    ->      [ 0.  0.  1.]
['code']     ->      [ 1.  0.  0.]
```

Implementation of the one-hot model is shown here:

```
# define input string
data = 'the quick brown fox jumped over the lazy dog'
consecutive_words = data.split()
print(data)

# construct the dictionary
all_words = list(set(consecutive_words))

# define a mapping of word to integers
word_to_int = dict((w, i) for i, w in enumerate(all_words))
int_to_word = dict((i, w) for i, w in enumerate(all_words))
# integer encode input data
integer_encoded = [word_to_int[w] for w in consecutive_words]

# one hot encode
onehot_encoded = list()
for value in integer_encoded:
    letter = [0 for _ in range(len(all_words))]
    letter[value] = 1
    onehot_encoded.append(letter)
_ = [print(x) for x in onehot_encoded]

def argmax(vector):
    # since vector is actually a list and its one hot encoding hence the
    # maximum value is always 1
    return vector.index(1)

# invert encoding
inverted = int_to_word[argmax(onehot_encoded[0])]
print(inverted)
```

Although one-hot encoding is simple to understand and implement, there are a number of disadvantages associated with it:

- **Not a distributed representation**: The number of dimensions for each vector grows with the size of the vocabulary. The matrix that is formed is highly sparse—which means that most of the individual values are 0s. Hence, the matrix manipulations become computationally too expensive even for a corpus of normal size.
- **Out-of-vocabulary words**: It is not able to handle new words at test time.
- **Not a distributional representation**: In one-hot encoding, all the vectors are equidistant from each other.

Bag of words

The bag of words model is concerned about whether known words occur in the document and only the frequency of the tokens in the document will be taken into account. So to create the document matrix using the bag of words approach, the following algorithm is used:

1. Find the number of separate words that are used in all the documents. Words are identified using spaces and punctuation as the separators.
2. Using the tokens, a feature space is created. For each document, each feature value is the count of the number of times the feature is present in the document. Hence, each row in the resultant matrix will correspond to each document. Count the number of tokens in each document. This is because each document will generate its own vector.
3. Normalize the vectors.

For example, let's say that there are two documents comprising the whole corpus:

```
Document1: "John likes to watch movies. Mary likes too."
Document2: "John also likes to watch football games."
```

So for all the sentences, our vocabulary is as follows:

```
['also', 'football', 'games', 'john', 'likes', 'mary', 'movies', 'to',
'too', 'watch']
```

To get the bag of words, we count the number of times each word occurs in the sentence. So the following are the vectors formed for each document:

```
Document1: {'likes': 2, 'John': 1, 'to': 1, 'watch': 1, 'movies': 1,
'Mary': 1, 'too': 1}
Document2: {'John': 1, 'also': 1, 'likes': 1, 'to': 1, 'watch': 1,
'football': 1, 'games': 1}
```

The main disadvantage of the bag of words approach is that the context of the word is lost. You can think of examples such as "Toy Dog" and "Dog Toy", which do not mean the same thing but will share the same vector. A simple implementation of bag of words is shown here:

```
import collections, re
texts = ['John likes to watch movies. Mary likes too.', 'John also likes to
watch football games.']
bagsofwords = [collections.Counter(re.findall(r'\w+', txt)) for txt in
texts]
```

```
print(bagsofwords[0])
print(bagsofwords[1])
sumbags = sum(bagsofwords, collections.Counter())
print(sumbags)
```

TF-IDF

Just counting the number of tokens in a document may not give sufficient information about the whole corpus. The idea is that rarer words give more information about what the document is about. In TF-IDF, the term frequency is normalized by the document frequency. The intuition is that TF-IDF makes rare words more prominent and scales down the effect of common words.

N-grams

N-gram-based approaches are based on Zipf's law which states the following:

> *The nth most common word in a human language text occurs with a frequency inversely proportional to n.*

In all languages, there are some words that are used more commonly than the others. The difference between more common words and less common words is not drastic but continuous. Another good corollary of this law is that if a class of documents corresponding to a specific frequency gets cut off, that will not massively affect the n-gram frequency profile. Hence, if we are comparing documents of the same category, they should have similar frequency profile.

N-grams frequency means the frequency of overlapping sequence of words. Here is a quote:

> *"Even now They talked in Their tombs."*
>
> *- H.P. Lovecraft*

From this sentence you can obtain the following n-grams. "_" is to show the start and end of the sentence:

- **1-grams (unigrams)**: Even, now, They, talked, in, Their, tombs (number of features: 7).
- **2-grams (bigrams)**: (_, Even), (Even, now), (now, They), (They, talked), (talked, in), (in, Their), (Their, tombs), (tombs, _) (number of features: 8).
- **3-grams (trigrams)**: (_, _, Even), (_, Even, now), (Even, now, They), (now, They, talked), (They, talked, in), (talked, in, Their), (in, Their, tombs), (Their, tombs, _), (tombs, _, _) (features: 9).

- **4-grams (trigrams)**: (_, _, _, Even), (_, _, Even, now), (_, Even, now, They), (Even, now, They, talked), (now, They, talked, in), (They, talked, in, Their), (talked, in, Their, tombs), (in, Their, tombs, _), (Their, tombs, _, _), (tombs, _, _, _) (features: 10).

And so on.

When dealing with only unigrams, the probability of the whole sentence can be written as follows:

```
P("Even now They talked in Their tombs.") = P("Even") * P("now") *
P("They") * P("talked") * P("in") * P("Their") * P("tombs")
```

Similarly, in the case of bigrams, the probability of the whole sentence can be written as follows:

```
P("Even now They talked in Their tombs.") = P("Even" | start of sentence) *
("now" | "Even") * ("They" | "now") * ("talked" | "They") * ("in" |
"talked") * ("Their" | "in") * ("tombs" | "Their") * (end of sentence |
"tombs")
```

As per maximum likelihood estimation, the conditional probability of something like P("now" | "Even") can be given as the ratio of count of the observed occurrence of "Even now" together by the count of the observed occurrence of "Even". This probability model can now be used to predict new sentences.

Let's build a model in case of bigrams. This file has been taken from the servers of University of Maryland Institute for Advanced Computer Studies, http://www.umiacs. umd.edu/ or you can use your own corpus. Keep it in the data folder.

Now, the following command will remove the new lines, then squash all the consecutive spaces, then get all the bigrams and sort them as per frequency:

```
$ cat data/persuasion.txt | tr '\n' ' ' | tr -s ' ' | tr -sc 'A-Za-z'
'\012' |   sed -e '1!{$!p' -e '}' | paste -d' ' - - | sort | uniq -c | sort
-nr > data/persuasion_bigrams.txt
```

Now we can build a sentence generator using this n-grams file:

```
def get_next_word(ngram_file, word1=None, sentence_length=0):
    with open(ngram_file) as f:
        for line in f:
            _, w1, w2 = line.split()
            if word1 is None or word1 == w1:
                sentence_length -= 1
                word1 = w2
                return w1, word1, sentence_length
```

```
def build_sentence(ngram_file, sentence_length):
    first_word = None
    sentence = ''
    while sentence_length > 0:
        w1, first_word, sentence_length = get_next_word(ngram_file,
first_word, sentence_length)
        sentence = sentence + ' ' + w1
    final_sentence = sentence + ' ' + first_word + '.'
    return final_sentence

print(build_sentence('data/persuasion_bigrams.txt', 10))
```

Using this n-gram sentence builder, we get the following sentence:

```
$ python build_sentence_ngrams.py
 of the same time to be a very well as she.
```

If this fascinates you, then try to build with trigrams or more.

The major drawback of n-grams is that they are extremely sparse and are not able to distinguish when encountering new words in the test data.

Model architecture in fastText

FastText models are a little bit different depending on whether they are unsupervised models or supervised models. In this chapter, we will mostly look at the unsupervised model.

The unsupervised model

In fastText, you can have the option to use two model architectures for computing a distributed representation of words. They are skipgram and CBOW. The model architectures used in fastText are both distributed architectures. So the aim is to learn a high-dimensional dense representation for each vocabulary term. The representation should be distributional as well as it tries to learn from context.

In both the architectures, you train a two-layer, shallow neural network to construct the context of words.

Skipgram

In skipgram, a context window of k is considered. All the other positions are skipped and only the relationship between the panel and the word is explored. This is done by feeding a one-hot encoding of the word to a two-layer shallow neural network. Since the input is one-hot encoded, the hidden layer consists of only one row of input hidden weight matrix. The task for the neural network is to predict the ith context given the word:

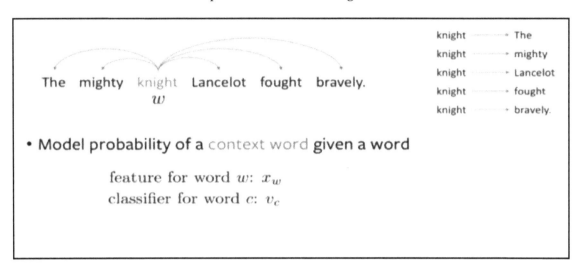

The scores for each word are computed using the following equation:

$$u = W'^T h \tag{1}$$

Here, h is a vector in the hidden layer and W is the hidden output weight matrix. After computing u, c multinomial weight distributions are computed, where c is the window size. The distributions are computed using the following equation:

$$p(w_{c,j} = w_{O,c}|w_I) = \frac{\exp u_{c,j}}{\sum_{j'=1}^{V} \exp u_{j'}} \tag{2}$$

Here, $w_{c,j}$ is the *j*th word on the *c*th panel of the output layer; $w_{O,c}$ is the actual *c*th word in the output context words; w_I is the only input word; and $u_{c,j}$ is the net input of the *j*th unit on the *c*th panel of the output layer. So you can see this is, in effect, trying to predict the context words given the input word. The probability is then converted into a softmax. If you try to visualize the above architecture, this should translate to something like the following:

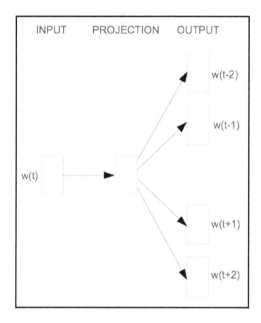

In addition, more distant words are given less weight-age by randomly sampling them. When you give the window size parameter, only the maximum window size is configured. In effect, the actual window size is randomly chosen between 1 and the maximum window size for each training sample. Thus the words that are the farthest are chosen with the probability of $1/c$, whereas the nearest words are always chosen.

Subword information skipgram

The skipgram model was taken in its original form from the word2vec implementation. The skipgram model is effective because it emphasizes the specific word and the word that comes along with it. But along with the specific word, the character of the n-grams may also have a lot of information. This is especially true of languages which are morphologically rich. In fastText, the authors took the skipgram implementation in word2vec, which is simply taking the vector representation of the whole word, and said that the vector representation of the word is actually the sum of the vector representations of the n-grams. Hence, in fastText, the scoring function (u) that you saw earlier is actually changed to the following:

$$s(w, c) = \sum_{g \in G_w} z_g^T V_c \tag{3}$$

SCORE = [3-6 char level n-grams] + [word]

In the library, n-grams for n greater or equal to 3 and less or equal to 6 is taken along with the word. So for something like `Schadenfreude` the collection of n-grams taken are as follows:

```
"shadenfreude" = {"sha", "had", "ade", ..., "shad", "frue", ..., "freude",
..., "shadenfreude"}
```

The major advantage of this method is that in the case of out-of-vector words, the [word] vector is not present and hence the score function transforms to the following:

SCORE = [3-6 char level n-grams]

Implementing skipgram

Now let's try to understand the skipgram method through some Python code. The Keras library has a very good and easy to understand skipgram function that you can see and understand how the skipgram should be implemented. For code in this section, you can take a look at the `fasttext skipgram cbow.ipynb` notebook which is inspired by the Keras implementations.

As discussed in skipgram, the task for the model is to predict the *i*th context given the word. How this is achieved in practice is by taking pairs of words from the document and then saying output is 1 in case the second word is the context word.

Now, given a sequence or an individual document (which, in this case, is probably a particular sentence), first create two lists: `couples` and `labels`. Now, for each target word, get the context window and in the context window for each combination of target word and context word, capture the combination in the `couples` list, and capture the label in the `labels` list:

```
couples = []
labels = []
for i, wi in enumerate(sequence):
    if not wi:
        continue

    window_start = max(0, i - window_size)
    window_end = min(len(sequence), i + window_size + 1)
    for j in range(window_start, window_end):
        if j != i:
            wj = sequence[j]
            if not wj:
                continue
            couples.append([wi, wj])
            if categorical:
                labels.append([0, 1])
            else:
                labels.append(1)
```

Since we have captured only positive values right now, we will need to capture some negative cases as well to train the model effectively. In the negative sampling case, for the number of negative samples, randomly generate some out-of-context word indexes with the target words that we have:

```
num_negative_samples = int(len(labels) * negative_samples)
words = [c[0] for c in couples]
random.shuffle(words)

couples += [[words[i % len(words)],
            random.randint(1, vocabulary_size - 1)] # basically get some
out of context word indices
            for i in range(num_negative_samples)]
```

```
if categorical:
    labels += [[1, 0]] * num_negative_samples # opposite of what you would
define for positive samples
else:
    labels += [0] * num_negative_samples
```

You can encapsulate the previous logic in a function, as has been done in the Keras function skipgrams and then return the combinations (denoted by the couples list) and the labels. This will be then passed on to the neural network, which will train on these combinations and corresponding labels:

```
for _ in range(epochs):
    loss = 0.
    for i, doc in enumerate(tokenizer.texts_to_sequences(corpus)):
        data, labels = skipgrams(sequence=doc, vocabulary_size=V,
window_size=5, negative_samples=5.)
        x = [np.array(x) for x in zip(*data)]
        y = np.array(labels, dtype=np.int32)
        if x:
            loss += model.train_on_batch(x, y)

    print(loss)
```

The skipgram model is essentially a hidden layer sandwiched between an input layer and the output layer. We can create a simple Keras model to capture that:

```
embedding_dim = 100

# inputs
w_inputs = Input(shape=(1, ), dtype='int32')
w = Embedding(V, embedding_dim)(w_inputs)

# context
c_inputs = Input(shape=(1, ), dtype='int32')
c = Embedding(V, embedding_dim)(c_inputs)
o = Dot(axes=2)([w, c])
o = Reshape((1,), input_shape=(1, 1))(o)
o = Activation('sigmoid')(o)

ft_model = Model(inputs=[w_inputs, c_inputs], outputs=o)
# ft_model.summary()
ft_model.compile(loss='binary_crossentropy', optimizer='adam')

Image(model_to_dot(ft_model, show_shapes=True).create(prog='dot',
format='png'))
```

This creates the following model:

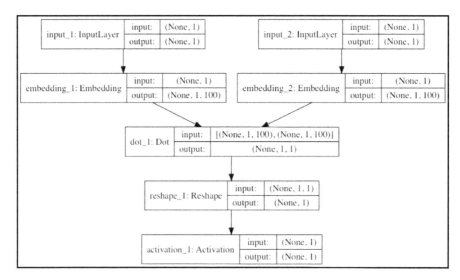

Finally, once the model is trained, we get the vectors from the trained weights of the embedding dimension:

```
with open('vectors.txt' ,'w') as f:
    f.write('{} {}\n'.format(V-1, embedding_dim))
    vectors = ft_model.get_weights()[0]
    for word, i in tokenizer.word_index.items():
        f.write('{} {}\n'.format(word, ' '.join(map(str, list(vectors[i,
:]))))))
```

Now we can save the vectors in our file and load them up when necessary.

CBOW

CBOW is the opposite of skipgram, where the specific word is taken as the target given the context. The number of words that are used as context words depends on the context word. So in this case, taking the previous example "Even now They talked in Their tombs", we can take the whole context `["Even" "now" "They" "in" "Their" "tombs."]` and generate the word "talked" from it.

So the algorithm is to take the one-hot vectors of all the words since now we are taking all the context words as the input. Considering that the window size is k, there will be 2 million one-hot vectors. Then take the embedding words vectors for all the words. Average out the word vectors to get the cumulative context. The output of the hidden layer is thus generated using the following equation:

$$h = \frac{1}{C}W \cdot (\sum_{i}^{C} x_i) \qquad (4)$$

It is worth noting that the hidden layer is one of the main differences between skipgram and CBOW in terms of being mirror images of one another.

Generate the score with the same score function as we saw when defining skipgram. The equation is almost the same except that since we are predicting all the words in the output based on the context, hence u and v for the different columns (denoted by j) needs to be computed:

$$u_j = v_{w_j}^T \cdot h \qquad (5)$$

Turn the score into probabilities using the softmax. Now we need to train this model so that the probabilities match the true probabilities of the word, which is the one-hot encoding of the actual word:

$$y_j = p(w_{y_i}|w_1, \ldots, w_c) = \frac{exp(u_j)}{\sum_{j=1}^{V} exp(u_j')} \qquad (6)$$

The CBOW architecture looks something like the following:

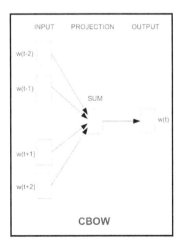

CBOW implementation

CBOW implementation is easier to code than skipgram as the `cbow` method is pretty much straightforward. For each target word, you take the context and try to predict the target word, keeping the context as the input.

Hence, for the implementation perspective, writing code for CBOW is simpler. For each word in the sequence, the same labels lists will be created but this list will be the actual target word under focus. The other list is the context list which will have the context words depending on the window. Now, once the input and output are fixed, we can then yield them so that the model can train on it:

```
def generate_data_for_cbow(corpus, window_size, V):
    maxlen = window_size*2
    corpus = tokenizer.texts_to_sequences(corpus)
    for words in corpus:
        L = len(words)
        for index, word in enumerate(words):
            contexts = []
            labels = []
            s = index - window_size
            e = index + window_size + 1
            contexts.append([words[i] for i in range(s, e) if 0 <= i < L
and i != index])
            labels.append(word)
            x = sequence.pad_sequences(contexts, maxlen=maxlen)
            y = np_utils.to_categorical(labels, V)
            yield (x, y)
```

The output of the preceding model will be in terms of NumPy vectors which can be passed to a keras model for batch training, similar to what you saw in the *Implementing skipgram* section. Here, `cbow` is the Keras model:

```
for ite in range(5):
    loss = 0.
    for x, y in generate_data_for_cbow(corpus, window_size, V):
        loss += cbow.train_on_batch(x, y)

    print(ite, loss)
```

For the CBOW model, you will need to define a input layer first. The embedding layer can be the average of the embedding layer, which is then passed on to an output layer using the `softmax` function. Hence we have the following:

```
cbow = Sequential()
cbow.add(Embedding(input_dim=V, output_dim=embedding_dim,
input_length=window_size*2))
```

```
cbow.add(Lambda(lambda x: K.mean(x, axis=1),
output_shape=(embedding_dim,)))
cbow.add(Dense(V, activation='softmax'))
```

You should see the following architecture being built:

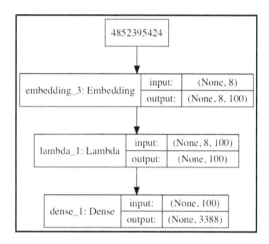

Run the code in the `fasttext skipgram cbow.ipynb` notebook. You will be able to compare the vectors created using skipgram and CBOW.

Comparison between skipgram and CBOW

Now, you might be wondering which architecture should be used more during the actual training of data. The following are some guidelines for differentiating between CBOW and skipgram when choosing to train the data:

- Skipgram works well with a small amount of training data. It works well even on rare words and phrases.
- CBOW is faster to train than skipgram. It also has higher accuracy on frequent words and phrases.

Loss functions and optimization

Choosing a loss function and an optimizing algorithm along with it is one of the fundamental strategies of machine learning. Loss functions are a way of associating a cost with the difference between the present model and the actual data distribution. The idea is that for specific loss function, optimizing algorithm pair, it would be possible to optimize the parameters of the model to make them mimic the real data as closely as possible.

Language models that use the neural probabilistic networks are generally trained using the maximum likelihood principle. The task is to maximize the probability of the next word w_t, which is taken as the target, given the previous words h which is the "history". We can model that in terms of the softmax function that we will discuss next.

Softmax

The most popular methods for learning parameters of a model is using gradient descent. Gradient descent is basically an optimization algorithm that is meant for minimizing a function, based on which way the negative gradient points toward. In machine learning, the input function that gradient descent acts on is a loss function that is decided for the model. The idea is that if we move towards minimizing the loss function, the actual model will "learn" the ideal parameters and will ideally generalize to out-of-sample or new data to a large extent as well. In practice, it has been seen this is generally the case and stochastic gradient, which is a variant of gradient descent, has a fast training time as well.

For the gradient descent to be effective, we need such an optimizing function that is convex and we want the logarithm of the model's output to be well behaved for gradient-based optimization of the likelihood, going with the **maximum likelihood estimation** (**MLE**) principle. Now, consider the fact that taking the logarithm of a series of products transforms it to a series of additions, and because the likelihood for the whole training dataset is actually the product of the individual likelihoods of each sample, it is easier to maximize the log-likelihood as this would mean that you are optimizing the sum of the log-likelihood of each sample indexed by k:

$$argmax_\theta \sum_{k=1}^{m} \log(P(y^{(k)}|x^{(k)};\theta)) \tag{7}$$

Now we need to chose a suitable function for determining the probabilities, given by P in this case. There are some good functions out there that can be used and one popular function is the sigmoid function. The sigmoid function looks like an S:

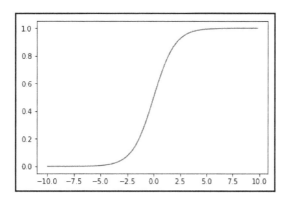

The sigmoid function is best used for binary classification tasks and is used in logistic regression.

Since we need to obtain the posterior distribution of words, our problem statement is more of a multinomial distribution instead of a binary one. Hence, we can chose the softmax distribution, which is a generalization of the sigmoid for the multi-class problem.

The softmax function calculates the probabilities distribution of the event over n different events. The softmax takes a class of values and converts them to probabilities with sum 1. So you can say that it is effectively squashing a k-dimensional vector of arbitrary real values to k-dimensional vector of real values within the range 0 to 1. The function is given by the following equation:

$$softmax(z) = \frac{exp(z)}{\sum_{k=1}^{K} exp(z_k)} \qquad (8)$$

You can use the following code to see what the softmax function looks like:

```
import numpy as np
import matplotlib.pyplot as plt
def softmax(arr):
    return np.exp(arr)/float(sum(np.exp(arr)))
def line_graph(x, y, x_title, y_title):
    plt.plot(x, y)
    plt.xlabel(x_title)
    plt.ylabel(y_title)
    plt.show()
graph_x = range(10)
graph_y = softmax(graph_x)
print('Graph X readings: {}'.format(graph_x))
print('Graph Y readings: {}'.format(graph_y))
line_graph(graph_x, graph_y, 'Inputs', 'softmax scores')
```

If you run the previous code in a Jupyter notebook, you should see a graph similar to the following. You can also see this in the `softmax function.ipynb` notebook under `chapter 3` folder:

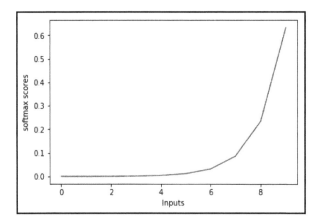

Note that as the values are higher, the probabilities are also higher. This is an interesting property of softmax, that is, the reaction to low stimuli is a rather uniform distribution and the reaction to high stimuli is probabilities that are closer to 0 and 1. If you are wondering why that is the case, this is because of the impact of the exponential function, which focuses on the extreme values.

So, for a given input word, this function will calculate the probabilities of each word over all possible words. If you train using the softmax function, the probability associated with the actual word should be the highest:

$$P(w_t|h) = softmax(score(w_t, h))$$

$$= \frac{exp(score(w_t, h)}{\sum_{Wordw' inVocab} exp(score(w_t, h))}$$

Here, the score function can be considered to be the compatibility of the word w_t with the context h.

Since we are training this model using the negative log likelihood on the training set:

$$J = -\log P(w_t|h)$$

$$= -score(w_t, h) + \log(\sum_{Wordw' inVocab} exp(score(w', h)).$$

Now we need to learn our softmax model using gradient descent and hence we need to compute the gradient with respect to the input words:

$$\nabla_{w_j} J(w)$$

The update of the parameter models will be in the opposite direction to the gradient:

$$w_j^{new} = w_j^{old} - \eta \cdot \nabla_{w_j} J(w)$$

In our context, let the vocabulary be V and the hidden layer size be N. The units on the adjacent layer are fully connected. The input is a one-hot encoded vector, which means for a given word input word context, only one out of the V units, $\{x_1, x_2, ..., x_V\}$, will be 1, and all other units are 0.

The weights between the input layer and output layer can be represented by a V x N matrix W. Each row of W is the N-dimensional vector representation v_w of the associated word of the input layer. Formally, row i of W is v_w^T. Given a context, assuming x_k=1 for a specific context word and 0 otherwise, we have the following:

$$h = W^T x = W_k^T$$

This is essentially the kth row of W. Lets call this v_{wI}. From the hidden layer to the output matrix, there is a different weight $W' = \{w_{ij}'\}$, which is a N x V matrix. Using these weights, you can compute a score u_j for each word in the vocabulary:

$$u_j = v_{w_j}'^T h$$

Here, $v_{w'j}$ is the *jth* column of the matrix W'. Now, using the softmax equation, we can obtain the following:

$$P(w_j|w_I) = \frac{exp(v'^T_{w_j} v_{w_I})}{\sum_{j'=1}^{V} exp(v'^T_{w_j} v_{w_I})}$$

v_w and v_w' are two representations of the word w. v_w comes from rows of W, which is the input to hidden weight matrix, and v_w' comes from columns of W', which is the hidden output matrix. In subsequent analysis, we will call v_w the "input vector" and v_w' the "output vector" of the word w. Considering u_j as the score as described, we can transform the loss function to equation (6) to the one as follows:

$$J = u_j - \log(\sum_i u_i)$$

Hierarchical softmax

Finding the softmax is highly computationally intensive. For each training instance, we have to iterate through every word in the vocabulary and compute the softmax. Thus, it is impractical to scale up to large vocabularies and large training corpora. To solve this problem, there are two approaches that are used in fastText: the hierarchical softmax and the negative sampling approach. We will discuss hierarchical softmax in this section and will discuss negative sampling in the next section. In both the approaches, the trick is to recognize that we don't need to update all the output vectors per training instance.

In hierarchical softmax, a binary tree is computed to represent all the words in the vocabulary. The *V* words must be leaf units of the tree. It can be proved that there are *V-1* inner units. For each unit, there exists a unique path from the root of the tree to the unit, and this path is used to estimate the probability of the word represented in the leaf unit:

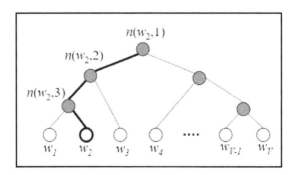

Each of the words can be reached by a path from the root through the inner nodes, which represent probability mass along the way. Those values are produced by the usage of simple sigmoid function as long as the path we are calculating is simply the product of those probability mass functions defined with the following:

$$\rho(x) = \frac{1}{1 + exp(-x)}$$

What is x in our specific case? It is calculated with the dot product of input and output vector representations of the word we are working with:

$$x = u_{n(w,j)} = v_{n(w,j)}^T v_{wI}$$

Here, $n(w, j)$ is the jth node on the path from the root to w.

In the hierarchical softmax model, there is no output representation of words. Instead, each of the V - 1 inner units has an output vector $v_{n(w,j)}'$. And the probability of a word being the output word is defined as follows:

$$P(w = w_O) = \prod_{j=1}^{L(w)-1} \rho(\|n(w, j+1) = ch(n(w, j))\| \cdot v_{n(w,j)}^T h)$$

Here, $ch(n)$ is the left child of unit n; $v_{n(w,j)}'$ is the vector representation ("output vector") of the inner unit $n(w,j)$; h is the output value of the hidden layer (in the skipgram model $h = v_\omega$

$$h = \frac{1}{C} \sum_{c=1}^{C} v_{w_c}$$

and in CBOW,   ); $\|x\|$ is a special function defined as follows:

$$\|x\| = \begin{cases} 1 \text{ if x is true.} \\ -1 \text{ otherwise.} \end{cases}$$

To calculate the probability of any output word, we need the probabilities of each intermediate node in the path from the root to the output word.

We define the probability of going right at an intermediate node as follows:

$$p(n, right) = \rho(v_n'^T) \cdot h$$

Since we are computing a binary tree, the probability of going left will be as follows:

$$p(n, left) = 1 - p(n, right)$$

Theoretically one can use many different types of trees for hierarchical softmax. You can randomly generate the tree. Or you can use existing linguistic resources such as WordNet. Morin and Benzio used this and showed that there was a 258x improvement over the randomly generated tree. But the nodes in the trees built this way generally have more than one edge. Another strategy is to learn the hierarchy using a recursive partitioning strategy or clustering strategy. The clustering algorithm can be a greedy approach, as shown in *Self-organized Hierarchical Softmax* by Yikang Shen, Shawn Tan, Christopher Pal, and Aaron Courville. We have another option in the form of Huffman codes, which are traditionally used in data compression circles. Since we are quite interested in clustering the documents by Nikhil Pawar, 2012, it is seen that when Huffman encoding is used to encode strings to integers, the clustering on the integer instances is much more effective. In word2vec and fastText, the Huffman tree is used. An interesting property of Huffman trees is that while an inner unit of a binary tree may not always have both children, a binary Huffman tree's inner units always do:

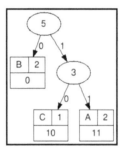

Tree generated using http://huffman.ooz.ie/?text=abcab

When building a Huffman tree, codes are assigned to the tokens such that the length of the code depends on the relative frequency or weight of the token. For example, in the previous example, the code for word E is 0000, which is one of the highest, and hence you can think that this word has occurred the most number of times in the corpus.

The code to build the tree can be found at `https://github.com/facebookresearch/fastText/blob/d72255386b8cd00981f4a83ae3 46754697a8f4b4/src/model.cc#L279`.

You can find the python implementation as part of the `Vocab` class in the method `encode_huffman`. For a simpler implementation, you can find the python implementation in the `huffman coding.ipynb` notebook in `chapter3` folder of the repository.

For the update equations, the computational complexity per training instance reduces from *O(V)* to *O(log(V))*, which is a huge improvement in terms of speed. We still roughly have the same number of parameters (*V-1* vectors for the inner units as compared to originally *V* output vectors for words).

 Google Allo uses hierarchical softmax layer to make their phrase recommendation faster.

Negative sampling

An alternative to the hierarchical softmax is **noise contrast estimation** (NCE), which was introduced by Gutmann and Hyvarinen and applied to language modeling by Mnih and Teh. NCE posits that a good model should be able to differentiate data from noise by means of logistic regression.

While NCE can be shown to approximate the log probability of the softmax, the skipgram model is only concerned with the learning high-quality vector representations, so we are free to simplify NCE as long as the vector representations retrain their quality. We define negative sampling by the following objective:

$$\log \rho(\nu_{wO}^T \nu_{\omega 1}) + \sum_{i=1}^{k} E_{w_i \sim P_n(\omega)} \left[\log(-\nu'_{wi} \nu_{\omega I}) \right]$$

This is used to replace the $log(P(W_O \mid W_I))$ term in the skipgram objective. Thus, the task is to distinguish the target word w_O from draws from the noise distribution $P_n(w)$ using logistic regression, where there are *k* negative samples for each data sample. In fastText, five negatives are sampled by default.

Subsampling of frequent words

In a very large corpus, the most frequent words can easily occur hundreds of millions of times, for example, words such as "in", "the" and "a". Such words generally provide less information value than the rare words. You can easily see that while the fastText model benefits from observing co-occurrences of "France" and "Paris", it benefits much less from observing co-occurrences of "France" and "the", as nearly every word co-occurs frequently within a sentence with "the". The idea can also be applied in the opposite direction. The vector representations of frequent words do not change significantly after training on several million additional examples.

To counter the imbalance between the rare and frequent words, we use a simple subsampling approach: each word w_i in the training set is discarded with the probability computed by the following formula:

$$P(w_i) = 1 - \sqrt{\frac{t}{f(w_i)}}$$

Here, the function f is the frequency of the ith word w and t is a chosen threshold and hence a hyperparameter. In fastText, the default value of t is chosen to be 0.0001. The code for this can be found at `https://github.com/facebookresearch/fastText/blob/53dd4c5cefec39f4cc9f988f9f39ab55eec6a02f/src/dictionary.cc#L281`.

Context definitions

Generally speaking, for a sentence of n words $w_1, w_{2, \dots,} w_n$ contexts of a word w_i comes from window of size k around the word:

$$C(w) = w_{i-k}, \dots, w_{i-1}, w_{i+1}, \dots, w_{i+k}$$

Here, k is a parameter. However there are two subtleties:

- **Dynamic window size**: The window size that is being used is dynamic—the parameter k denotes the maximal window size. For each word in the corpus, a window size k' is sampled uniformly from 1,...,k.
- **Effect of subsampling and rare word pruning**: Similar to word2vec, fastText has two additional parameters for discarding some of the input words: words appearing less frequently than `minCount` are not considered as either words or contexts, and in addition, frequent words (as defined by the -t parameter) are down sampled. Importantly, these words are removed from the text before generating the contexts. This has the effect of increasing the effective window size for certain words. Subsampling of frequent words should improve the quality of the resultant embeddings.

Summary

In this chapter, you have taken a look at unsupervised learning in fastText, as well as the algorithms and methods that enable it.

The next chapter will be about how fastText has approached supervised learning and you will also learn about how model quantization works in fastText.

4
Sentence Classification in FastText

In this chapter, we will cover the following topics:

- Sentence classification
- fastText supervised learning:
    - Architecture
    - Hierarchical softmax architecture
    - N-grams features and the hashing trick:
        - The **Fowler-Noll-Vo (FNV)** hash
    - Word embeddings and their use in sentence classification
- fastText model quantization:
    - Compression:
        - Quantization
        - Vector quantization:
            - Finding the codebook for high-dimensional spaces
        - Product quantization
        - Additional steps

Sentence classification

Sentence classification deals with understanding text found in natural languages and determining the classes that it may belong to. In the text classification set of problems, you will have a set of documents d that belongs to the corpus X (which contains all the documents). You will also have a set of finite classes $C = \{c_1, c_2, ..., c_n\}$. Classes are also called categories or labels. To train a model, you would need a classifier, which is generally a well-tested algorithm (not necessary but in this case we will be talking about a well-tested algorithm that is used in fastText) and you will need a corpus with documents and associated labeling identifying the classes that each document belongs to.

Text classification has many practical uses, such as the following:

- Creating spam classifiers in email
- Page ranking and indexing in search engines
- Sentiment detection in reviews that will give an idea whether customers are happy with the product or not

Text classification is generally a way to augment manual classification. Labeling a document is largely subjective and depends on the corpus. A sample document "I like traveling to Hawaii" may be regarded as falling under the class "Travel" by a librarian but may be regarded as "Irrelevant" by a doctor. So the idea is that a set of documents will be labeled by a domain expert, the labeled data will be used to train a text classifier, and then the text classifier can be used to predict new incoming text, saving the time and resources of the domain expert (maybe the domain expert can periodically check and audit the performance of the classifier against incoming text). Also, the proposed idea is for general people and does not apply to crowd-sourced labeling as done by stack overflow when it asks for users to label; most business problems do not have the luxury of such *auto* labeling and hence you will have to spend some time manually labeling the documents.

To evaluate the performance of a classification model, we divide the training corpus into test and train sets. Only the train set is used for model training. Once done, we classify the test set and compare the predictions with the actual ones and measure the performance. The portion of correctly classified documents to the portion of actual documents is called accuracy. There are two more parameters that we can look at that will give a measure for the model performance. One is the *recall*, which means the percentage of all the correct labels that we recalled as opposed to the labels that actually existed. We can also look at the *precision* of the model, which means that we look at all the predicted labels and say which portions of them are the actual labels in the first place.

fastText supervised learning

A fastText classifier is built on top of a linear classifier, specifically a BoW classifier. In this section, you will get to know the architecture of the fastText classifier and how it works.

Architecture

You can consider that each piece of text and each label is actually a vector in space and the coordinates of that vector are what we are actually trying to tweak and train so that the vector for a text and associated label are really close in space:

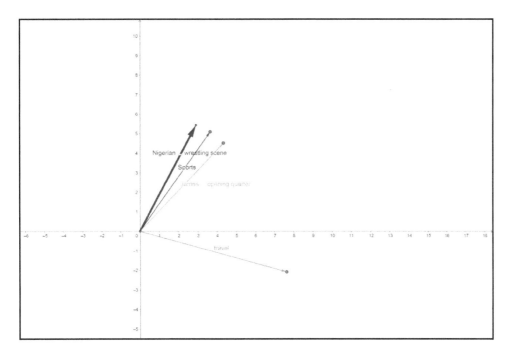

Vector representation of the text

So, in this example, which is an example shown in 2D space, you have texts that are saying things such as "Nigerian Tommy Thompson is also a relative newcomer to the wrestling scene" and "James scored 20 of his 46 points in the opening quarter" are closer to the "sports" label and not the "travel" label.

The way we can do this is we can take the vector representing the text and the vector representing the label and input it into the scoring function. We then take the score and then we normalize across sum of all the scores between the vector representing the text and the vector representations for every other possible label. And that provides us with the type of probability that the given text above will have the label. The scores are the individual values and we convert them to probabilities using the softmax function which was also discussed in the previous chapter.

The fastText uses similar vector space models for text classification, where the words are reduced to low-dimensional vectors called embeddings. The aim is to train and arrive at a vector space such that the sentence vectors and the label vectors are really close to each other. To apply vector space models to sentences or documents, one must first select an appropriate function, which is a mathematical process for combining multiple words.

Composition functions fall into two classes: unordered or syntactic. Unordered functions treat input texts as **bag of words** (**BoW**) embeddings, while syntactic representations take word order and sentence structure into account. The fastText is mostly an unordered approach since it takes the BoW approach but has a little bit of syntactic representations using the n-grams, as we will see later.

What you can do next is take the representations and then train a linear classifier on top of them. Good linear classifiers that can be used are logistic regression and **support vector machines** (**SVM**). Linear classifiers, though, have a little caveat. They do not share parameters between features and classes. As a result of this, there is a possibility that this limits the generalization capabilities to those types of classes which do not have many examples to train on. The solution to this problem is to use multilayered neural networks or to factorize the linear classifier into low rank matrices and then run a neural network on top of them.

Syntactic representations are more sparse than BoW approach and hence require more training time. This makes them computationally very expensive in case of huge datasets or when you have limited computational resources. For example, if you build a recursive neural network for training on syntactic word representations that again computes costly tensor products, and furthermore there will be non-linearity in every node of a syntactic parse tree, then your training time may stretch to days, which is prohibitive for fast feedback cycles.

So you can use an averaging network, which is an unordered model that can be explained in three simple steps:

1. Take the vector average of the embeddings associated with an input sequence of tokens.
2. Pass the average through one or more feed-forward layers.
3. Perform linear classification on the final layer's representation.

The model can be improved by applying a novel dropout-inspired regularizer. In this case, for each training instance, some of the token embeddings will be randomly dropped before computing the average. In fastText, this is done by subsampling frequent words, which was also discussed in the previous chapter and is used in the classifier as well.

A general form of the architecture is as follows:

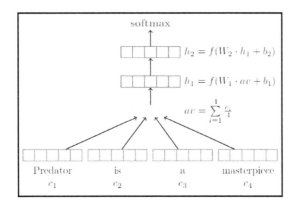

In this case, we want to map an input sequence of tokens to k labels. We first apply a composition function g to the sequence of word embeddings v_ω for $\omega \in X$. The output of this composition function is a vector z that serves as input to the logistic regression function. The architecture of the classification is similar to the cbow model that was discussed in the previous chapter.

First, a weighted average of the word embeddings is taken:

$$z = g(w \in X) = \frac{1}{|X|} \sum_{w \in X} \nu_\omega$$

Feeding z to a softmax layer induces estimated probabilities for each output label:

$$y = softmax(W_s \cdot z + b)$$

Here, the softmax function is as follows:

$$softmax(x) = \frac{exp(x)}{\sum_{k=1}^{K} exp(x_k)}$$

Here, W_s is a $k \times d$ matrix for the dataset with k output labels and b is a bias term. fastText uses a generic bias term in the form of an end of sentence character <s> that gets added to all input examples.

This model can then be trained to minimize cross-entropy error, which for a single training instance with ground truth label y is as follows:

$$l(\hat{y}) = \sum_{p-1}^{k} y_p \log(\hat{y}_p)$$

In fastText, this gets translated to computing the probability distribution over the predefined classes. For the set of N documents, this leads to minimizing the negative log likelihood over the classes:

$$-\frac{1}{N} \sum_{n=1}^{N} y_n \log(f(BAx_n))$$

Here, x_n is the normalized bag of features of the nth document, y_n is the label, and A and B are the weight matrices. A is just a lookup table over the words in fastText.

Then we can use stochastic gradient descent to keep tweaking those coordinates until we maximize the probability of the correct label for every piece of text. The fastText trains this model asynchronously on multiple CPUs using stochastic gradient descent and a linearly decaying learning rate.

The architecture that is used in fastText is as follows:

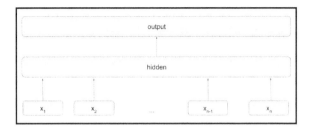

Model architecture of fastText for a sentence with N gram word features $x_1, x_2, ... x_N$. The features are embedded and averaged to form the hidden variable.

Now let's summarize the architecture:

- It starts with word representations, which are averaged into text representations, which are fed into a linear classifier
- The classifier is essentially a linear model with a rank constraint and fast loss approximation
- The text representation is a hidden state that can be shared among features and classes
- A softmax layer is used to obtain a probability distribution over predefined classes
- High computational complexity $O(kh)$, where k is the number of classes and h is the dimension of the text representation

Hierarchical softmax architecture

Finding the softmax is computationally quite expensive and prohibitive for a large corpus as this means that we not only have to find the score for the text with the label but the scores for the text with all the labels. So for n text and m labels, this scales with worst case performance of $O(n^2)$, which you know is not good.

Also, softmax and other similar methods for finding the probabilities do not take into account the semantically meaningful organization of classes. A classifier should know that classifying a dog as a submarine should have a higher penalty than a dog as a wolf. An intuition that we may have is that the target labels are probably not flat but rather a tree.

So now we have *k* classes that we want each input to be classified into. So let's consider these classes are the leaves of a tree. This tree is organized in such as way that the hierarchy is semantically meaningful. Consider further that our classifier maps an input to an output probability distribution over the leaves. Hopefully, this leaf will be the correct class of the corresponding input. The probability of any node in the tree is the probability of the path from the root to that node. If the node is at depth *l* + *1* with parents $n_1, n_2, ..., n_l$ then the probability of the node is as follows:

$$P(n_l + 1) = \prod_{i=1}^{l} P(n_i)$$

A leaf falls under the node if the node is on the path from the root to the leaf. We then define the amount of the "win" or the "winnings" to be the weighted sum of the probabilities of the nodes along its path from the root to the leaf corresponding to the correct classes. During the optimization or the training process, we want to maximize this "winnings" for our model, and conversely minimize the "loss". Loss in this case is considered the negative of the win.

So in fastText, what is used is the hierarchical classifier, which is similar to the hierarchical softmax that you saw in the earlier chapter. In this method, it represents the labels in a binary tree and so every node in the binary tree is represented as a probability and so a label is represented by the probability along the path to that given label. In this case, the correct label is generated using the **breadth first search** (**BFS**) algorithm. BFS is quite fast for searching and hence you bring down the complexity to $log_2 n$. Now we just need to compute the probabilities of the path to the correct label. So when we have a lot of labels, this really increases the speed of computation for all the labels and hence the model training. And as you have seen in the previous chapter, the hierarchical probability representation asymptotes to the softmax probabilities and hence this approximations actually give the same kind of model performance and are vastly faster to train.

As you have seen in the previous chapter, in this case the output of the hierarchical classifier is the label. Similar to training word embeddings, in this case a Huffman tree is formed. Since we have already discussed the internals of the Huffman tree in the previous chapter, in this case we will tinker at little bit with the code and try to see the exact tree that is formed and find the probabilities associated with it.

To keep things simple, we will take a very small dataset with very small number of labels. In this example, the following set of sentences along with the labels are taken and saved in a file named `labeledtextfile.txt`:

```
__label__sauce How much does potato starch affect a cheese sauce recipe?
```

```
    __label__food-safety Dangerous pathogens capable of growing in acidic
environments
    __label__restaurant Michelin Three Star Restaurant; but if the chef is not
there
    __label__baking how to seperate peanut oil from roasted peanuts at home?
    __label__baking Fan bake vs bake
    __label__sauce Regulation and balancing of readymade packed mayonnaise and
other sauces
```

Since fastText is written in C++, for performance reasons it does not manipulate and work with the direct label strings. To get the Huffman codes of the label, you can change the hierarchicalSoftmax function on line 81 of model.cc to the following:

```
real Model::hierarchicalSoftmax(int32_t target, real lr) {
  real loss = 0.0;
  grad_.zero();
  const std::vector<bool>& binaryCode = codes[target];

  std::cout << "\ntarget: " << target << ", vector: ";
  for (std::vector<bool>::const_iterator i = binaryCode.begin(); i !=
binaryCode.end(); ++i)
      std::cout << *i << ' ';
  std::cout << '\n';

  const std::vector<int32_t>& pathToRoot = paths[target];

  if (target == 0)
  {
      std::cout << "will check the path to root for bakings: " << ' ';
      for (int32_t i = 0; i < pathToRoot.size(); i++) {
          std::cout << pathToRoot[i] << '_' << "target_" << target <<
"_Individual loss_" << binaryLogistic(pathToRoot[i], binaryCode[i], lr) <<
' ';
      }
      std::cout << '\n';
  }

  if (target == 1)
  {
      std::cout << "will check the path to root for sauce: " << '\n';
      for (int32_t i = 0; i < pathToRoot.size(); i++) {
          std::cout << pathToRoot[i] << '_' << "target_" << target <<
"_Individual loss_" << binaryLogistic(pathToRoot[i], binaryCode[i], lr) <<
' ';
      }
      std::cout << '\n';
  }
```

```
if (target == 2)
{
    std::cout << "will check the path to root for sauce: " << '\n';
    for (int32_t i = 0; i < pathToRoot.size(); i++) {
        std::cout << pathToRoot[i] << '_' << "target_" << target <<
"_Individual loss_" << binaryLogistic(pathToRoot[i], binaryCode[i], lr) <<
' ';
    }
    std::cout << '\n';
}

if (target == 3)
{
    std::cout << "will check the path to root for restaurant: " << '\n';
    for (int32_t i = 0; i < pathToRoot.size(); i++) {
        std::cout << pathToRoot[i] << '_' << "target_" << target <<
"_Individual loss_" << binaryLogistic(pathToRoot[i], binaryCode[i], lr) <<
' ';
    }
    std::cout << '\n';
}

for (int32_t i = 0; i < pathToRoot.size(); i++) {
    loss += binaryLogistic(pathToRoot[i], binaryCode[i], lr);
}

// std::cout << "total loss for target: " << target << " is: " << loss;
// std::cout << '\n';

return loss;
}
```

As you can see, I am listing for multiple labels. But you can choose the label that you want. You will get output similar to this. You will need to get the last occurrence of the target value to get the vector:

```
target: 2, vector: 1 0 1
 will check the path to root for sauce:
 0_target_2_Individual loss_0.693147 1_target_2_Individual loss_0.681497
2_target_2_Individual loss_0.693147
```

So the similar vector, corresponding to target 2, is 101.

The n-gram features and the hashing trick

As you have seen, the BoW of the vocabulary is taken to arrive at the word representation to be used later in the classification process. But the BoW is unordered and does not have any syntactic information. Hence, the bag of n-grams are used as additional features to capture some of the syntactic information.

As we have already discussed, large-scale NLP problems almost always involve using a large corpus. This corpus will always have *unbounded* number of unique words, as we have seen from the Zipf's law. Words are generally defined as a string of characters separated with a delimiter, such as a space in English. Hence, taking word n-grams is simply not scalable to large corpora, which is essential to come to accurate classifications.

Because of these two factors, the matrices that are formed naively are always sparse and high-dimensional. You can try to reduce the dimensions of the matrices using techniques such as PCA but that would still involve doing matrix manipulations that require such a high amount of memory that it would make the whole computation infeasible.

What if you can do something so that you are able to circumvent the creation of the dictionary? A similar problem is tackled with what is known as the kernel trick. The kernel trick enables us to use linear classifiers on non-linear data. In this method, the input data is transformed to a high-dimensional feature space. Interestingly, you just need to specify the kernel for this step, no need to transform all the data to the feature space, and it will work. In other words, when you compute the distance and apply the kernel, you get a number. The number is the same as what you would have got if you expanded your initial points into the higher-order space that your kernel points to and computed their inner product:

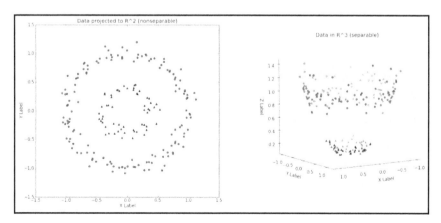

Source: https://towardsdatascience.com/understanding-the-kernel-trick-e0bc6112ef78

It's a lot easier to get the inner product in a higher-dimensional space than the actual points in the higher dimensional space.

The challenges of text classification are complementary. The original input space is generally linearly separable (because generally humans decide on the features based on tagging) but the training set is prohibitively large in size and very high-dimensional. For this common scenario, a complementary variation to the kernel trick is used. This method is called the hashing trick. Here, the high-dimensional vectors in $\mathfrak{R}^d$ are mapped into a lower-dimensional feature space $\mathfrak{R}^m$ such that $m \ll d$. We will train the classifier in $\mathfrak{R}^m$ space.

The core idea in the hashing trick is the hash functions. So in text classification and similar NLP tasks, we take a non-cryptographic hash such as murmur or FNV (more on this later in the chapter) and map the work into a finite integer (usually 32-bit or 64-bit integers which are modulo of a prime number).

The following are some of the characteristics that define a hash function:

- The most important one—if you feed the same input to a hash function, it will always give the same output.
- The choice of the hash function determines the range of the possible outputs. The range is generally fixed. For example, modern websites use SHA256 hashes that are truncated to 128 bits.
- Hash functions are meant to be one way. Given a hash, the input should not be computable.

Due to the fact that they have a fixed range, a pleasant side effect of using hash functions is that there are fixed memory requirements. Another advantage is that we get benefits on the **out-of-vocabulary** (**OOV**) front as well. This part is not that obvious so let me explain it. The first step on that note is that we don't have to deal with the vocabulary at all. Instead, when starting with our BoW representations, we will start with a big column vector (2 million in our case) with a lot of elements for each of our training samples:

```
FastText is an open-source, free, lightweight library that allows users to
learn text representations and text classifiers
-> [0 0 0 0 ... 0 0 0 0] (2000000 elements)
```

Now we will choose a hash function *f* that takes in strings as inputs and outputs values. In other words, we are making sure that our hash function will never address an index outside our feature's dimensions.

There is the advantage in terms of OOV words as well, as compared to maintaining a large vocabulary in a *naive* BoW approach. Because the vector representation is created using a hash function, any string, even OOV words, will have a vector in the hash space. New words will worsen the accuracy of our classifier, true, but it will still work. No need to throw away the new words when predicting.

One reason why this should work comes from the same Zipf's law that we are time and again referring to. Hash collisions that may happen (if any), would probably be between infrequent words or between frequent word and an infrequent word. This is because frequent words by definition will occur earlier and hence tend to occupy the spaces first. Thus the collided feature used for classification will be either unlikely to be selected for feature selection or represent the word that led the classifier to select it.

Now that we have established the benefits of the hashing trick, we need to focus on the hashing function. There are many hash functions that are used for implementing the hashing trick, for example, Vowpal Wabbit and scikit-learn murmurhash v3. A good list of possible non-cryptographic hashes can be found at the following Wiki link: `https://en.wikipedia.org/wiki/List_of_hash_functions#Non-cryptographic_hash_functions`. FastText uses the FNV-1a hash, which will be discussed below.

The FNV hash

fastText uses the FNV-1a hash, which is the derivative of the FNV hash. To implement this algorithm, start with an initial hash value of `FNV_offset_basis`. For each byte in the input, take the XOR of the hash and the byte. Now multiply the result with the FNV prime. In terms of pseudo code:

```
hash = FNV_offset_basis
    for each byte_of_data to be hashed
        hash = hash XOR byte_of_data
        hash = hash × FNV_prime
    return hash
```

Source: Wikipedia, `https://en.wikipedia.org/wiki/Fowler%E2%80%93Noll%E2%80%93Vo_hash_function`

In fastText, this is implemented in the `dictionary.cc` hash function (`https://github.com/facebookresearch/fastText/blob/master/src/dictionary.cc#L143`):

```
uint32_t Dictionary::hash(const std::string& str) const {
  uint32_t h = 2166136261;
  for (size_t i = 0; i < str.size(); i++) {
```

```
        h = h ^ uint32_t(str[i]);
        h = h * 16777619;
    }
    return h;
}
```

As you can see, the offset basis considered is `2166136261` and corresponding prime number is `16777619`.

FNV is not cryptographic yet it has a high dispersion quality and a variable size hash result that can be any power of 2 from 32 to 1024 bits. The formula to generate it is among the simplest hash functions ever invented that actually achieve good dispersion. It also has good collision and bias resistance. One of the best properties of the FNV is that although it is not considered cryptographic, subverting bit sizes above 64 bits is mostly unsolvable. As the computational overhead needs to be kept to a minimum, fastText uses 32 bit, which has an FNV offset bias of 2166136261.

Take a look at the Python implementation in the file `fnv1a.py` under the `chapter4` folder in the repo.

In fastText, word- and character-level n-grams are hashed into a fixed number of buckets. This prevents the memory requirements when training the model. You can change the number of buckets using the `-buckets` parameter. By default, the number of buckets is fixed at 2M (2 million).

Word embeddings and their use in sentence classification

As you have seen in the previous chapter, word embeddings are the numerical representation of words in the shape of a vector in $\mathscr{R}^d$. They are unsupervised learned word representation vectors where there should be a correlation on semantic similarity. We also discussed what distributional representations and distributed representations are in `Chapter 7`, *Deploying Models to Web and Mobile*.

When performing sentence classification, there is the hypothesis that one can take an existing, near-state-of-the-art, supervised NLP system and improve it using word embeddings. You can either create your own unsupervised word embeddings using the fastText cbow/skipgram approach as shown in `Chapter 2`, *Creating Models Using FastText Command Line*, or you can download them from the `fasttext.cc` website.

A question that may arise is whether certain word representations are better for certain tasks. Present research on some specific areas shows that word representations that work well in some tasks do not work well in others. An example that is generally given is that word representations that work in named entity recognition tasks do not work well when the problem domain is search query classification and vice versa.

fastText model quantization

Due to the efforts of the Facebook AI Research team, there is a way to get vastly smaller models (in terms of the size that they take up in the hard drive), as you have seen in the *Model quantization* section in `Chapter 2`, *Creating Models Using FastText Command Line*. Models which take up hundreds of MBs can be quantized to only a couple of MBs. For example, if you see the DBpedia model released by Facebook, which can be accessed at the web page `https://fasttext.cc/docs/en/supervised-models.html`, notice that the regular model (this is the BIN file) is of 427 MB while the smaller model (the FTZ file) is only 1.7 MB.

This reduction in size is achieved by throwing out some of the information that is encoded in the BIN files (or the bigger model). The problem that needs to be solved here is how to keep information that is important and how to identify information that is not that important so that the overall accuracy and performance of the model is not compromised by a significant margin. In this section, we will take a look at the considerations for that.

Compression techniques

Since we are interested in understanding how to go about compressing the big fastText model files, let's take a look at some of the compression techniques that can be used.

Different compression techniques can be categorized as the following:

- **Lossless compression**: As the name suggests, lossless compression techniques are those techniques that will reproduce the same information structure when you compress, then uncompress. There is no loss in information. This type of compression is mostly done using statistical modeling. You have already encountered an algorithm that is used in this type of compression, namely Huffman coding.

- **Lossy compression**: Lossy compression is about discarding as much data as possible without discarding the benefits or usefulness of the data as much as possible. This is a good technique when we are not interested in recreating the original data, but more on what the original data represents. As you can correctly infer, you will generally be able to get a higher level of compression using lossy compression.

FastText employs a type of lossy compression known as product quantization. In the following sections, we will try to understand what quantization is, then how the idea of vector quantization comes from that and how it implements compression. Then we will take a look at how product quantization is a better variant of vector quantization for this task.

Quantization

The concept of quantization has been taken from the world of **digital signal processing** (**DSP**). In DSP, when converting an analog signal (for example, sound waves) into a digital signal, the signal is broken down to a series of individual samples based on a bit depth that determines the number of levels that the quantized signal will have. In the case of 8-bit quantization, you will have 2^8=256 possible combinations for the amplitude signal, and similarly, in 16-bit quantization, you will have 2^{16}=65536 possible combinations.

In the following example, a sine wave is quantized to 3-bit levels and hence it will support 8 values for the continuous sine wave. You can see the code to get the following image in the `product quantization.ipynb` notebook:

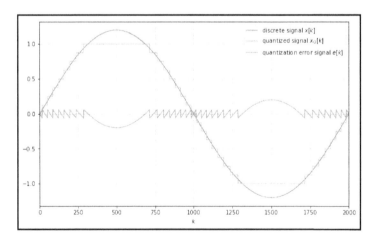

Vector quantization

Vector quantization is a technique to apply the ideas of quantization to vector spaces. Let's say that you have a vector space $\Re_k$ and a training set consisting of N samples of k-dimensional vectors on the target vector space. Vector quantization is the process where you map your vectors into a finite set of vectors Y, which are part of the target vector space. Each vector y_i is called a **code vector** or a **codeword** and the set of all *codewords* is called a **codebook**:

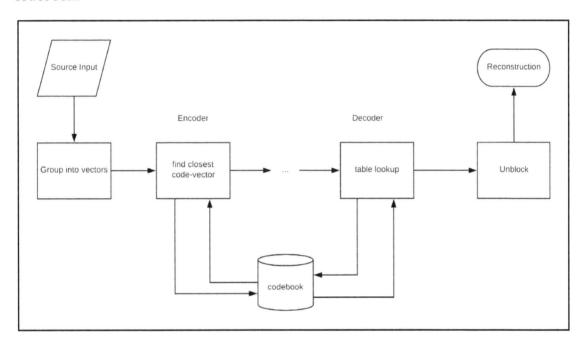

The amount of compression that is achieved is dependent on the size of the codebook. If we have a codebook of size k and the input vector is of dimension L, we need to specify $\log_2(k)$ bits to specify which of the codewords are selected from the codebook. Hence, the rate for an L-dimensional vector quantizer with a code book of size k is $\log_2 \dfrac{k}{L}$.

Let's understand how that happens in more detail. If you have a vector of L dimension where $L=8$, it is represented as follows:

$[0\ 1\ 2\ 3\ 4\ 5\ 6\ 7]$

Now there are 8 numbers and hence you need 3 bits to put it in memory in case you choose to encode in binary. Converting the array into binary you get the following vector:

[000 001 010 011 100 101 110 111]

So you need 24 bits to save the previous array in memory if you want to save each number as 3 bits. What if you want to reduce the amount of memory consumption of each number by 1 bit? If you are able to achieve that, you will be able to use only 16 bits to save the previous array in memory and thus save 8 bits, achieving compression. To do that, you can consider the numbers 0, 2, 4, 6 as your codebook which will maps to the vectors 00, 01, 10, 11:

0	2	4	8
00	01	10	11

During the transformation, all numbers between 0 and 2 are mapped to 00, everything from 2 to 4 is mapped to 01, and so on. Hence your original vector gets changed to the following:

0	1	2	3	4	5	6	7
00	00	01	01	10	10	11	11

The amount of space that this vector occupies in memory is only 8 bits.

Note that we can also target to encode our representation to 1 bit. In that case, only 2 bits of overall memory would be used for the array. But we lose more information about the original distribution. Hence, generalizing this understanding, decreasing the size of the codebook increases the compression ratio, but distortion of the original data increases.

Finding the codebook for high-dimensional spaces

The principal goal while designing for vector quantizers is to find a codebook, specifying a decoder, and a rule for specifying the encoder, such that the overall performance of the vector space is optimal.

An important class of quantizers is the Voronoi or nearest-neighbor quantizers. Given a set of L codevectors $C = |c_i|_{i=1,..L}$ of size N, along with a distance measure $d(x, y)|x, y \in R^k$, the R^k space is partitioned into L disjoint regions, known as Voronoi regions, with each codevector associated with each region. A particular Voronoi region Ω_j associated with the codevector v_j contains all the points in R^k space nearer to v_j than any other codevector and is the nearest-neighbor locus region of v_j. The following is an example Voronoi diagram for a given space with the associated codevectors denoted by points:

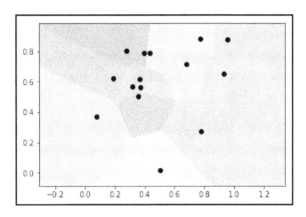

The code for getting the above diagram can also be found in the Jupyter notebook for the repo: https://github.com/PacktPublishing/Learn-fastText/blob/master/chapter4/product%20quantization.ipynb.

So, essentially, you can see that there are two steps to the process:

1. **Constructing the Voronoi space**: A preprocessing phase of constructing the Voronoi space, representing it in the form of a graph data structure and associating with each facet (for instance, vertex, edge, and region), the set of closest codevectors.
2. **Finding the codevector**: Given the Voronoi subdivisions, determine the facet of the subdivision which contains the query vector, and the associate code vector is the desired nearest neighbor.

Product quantization

Till now, you might have understood that in vector quantization, you cluster the search space into a number of bins based on the distance to the cluster centroid. If a query vector is quantized to that bin, all other vectors in the bin are good candidates.

Unfortunately, if a query lies at the edge, one has to consider all the neighboring bins as well. This might not seem a big deal until you realize that number of neighbors adjacent to each Voronoi cell increases exponentially with respect to the dimension N of the space. Note that when creating fastText vectors, we routinely deal in high dimensions such as 100, 300, and so on.

The default vectors in fastText are 100-dimensional vectors. A quantizer working on 50-bit codes, which means we only have a half (0.5) bit per component, contains $k = 2^{50}$ centroids (around 150 TB). Product quantization is an efficient solution to address this issue. The input vector x_i is divided into m distinct subvectors j $u_j, 1 \leq j \leq m$ of dimension $D^* = D/m$, where D is a multiple of m. The subvectors are quantized separately using m distinct quantizers. A given vector v is therefore mapped as follows:

$$\underbrace{x_1, \ldots, x_{D^*}}_{u_1(x)}, \ldots, \underbrace{x_{D-D^*+1}, \ldots, x_D}_{u_m(x)} \to q_1(u_1(x)), \ldots, q_m(u_m(x))$$

Here, q_j is a low-complexity quantizer associated with the jth subvector. With the subquantizer q_j, we associate the index I_j, the codebook C_j, and the corresponding reproduction values $c_{j,i}$.

A reproduction value of the **product quantizer** (**PQ**) is identified by an element of the product index set $I = I_1 \times I_2 \ldots \times I_m$. The codebook is therefore defined as the Cartesian product:

$$C = C_1 \times C_2 \times \ldots \times C_m$$

A centroid of this set is the concatenation of the centroids of the m sub-quantizers. From now on, we assume that all sub-quantizers have the same finite number k^* of reproduction values. In that case, the total number of centroids is given by the following:

$$k = (k^*)^m.$$

In fastText, the two parameters involved in product quantization, namely the number of sub-quantizers m and the number of bits b per quantization index, are typically set to $k \in [2, m/2]$, and b=8.

Thus, a PQ can generate an exponentially large codebook at very low memory/time cost. The essence of a PQ is to decompose the high-dimensional vector space into the Cartesian product of the subspaces and then quantize these subspaces separately. The optimal space decomposition is important for good product quantization implementation, and as per current knowledge, this is generally done by minimizing quantization distortions with respect to the space decomposition and quantization codebooks. There are two known ways to solve this optimization problem. One is using iterative quantization. A simple example of iteratively finding the codevectors is shown in the notebook, which can be considered a specific subquantizer. If you are interested, you can take a look at *Optimised Product Quantization* by Kaiming He et al.

The other method, and one which fastText adopts, is having a Gaussian assumption for the input vectors and finding the k-means through expectation maximization. Take a look at the algorithm in this k-means function: `src/productquantizer.cc#L115`.

After quantizing on the input matrix, retraining is done on the output matrix, keeping the input matrix the same. This is done so that the network readjusts to the quantization.

Additional steps

Following are the additional steps that can be taken:

- **Feature selection and pruning**: Pruning is done on those features that do not have a big influence on the decision of the classifier. During the classification step, only a limited number of K words and n-grams are selected. So for each document, first verification is done if it is covered by a retrained feature and, if not, we add the feature with the highest norm to the set of retrained features.
- **Hashing**: Both the words and n-grams are also hashed to further save on the memory.

If you decide to implement these techniques discussed in your own model compression methods, there are various ideas here that you can tweak and see if you get better performance in your particular domain:

- You can explore whether some other distance metrics makes sense for finding the k-means.
- You can change the pruning strategy based on neighborhood, entropy, and so on.

Summary

With this chapter, you have completed a deep dive into the theory behind how the fastText model is designed and implemented, the benefits, and the things that you need to consider while implementing it in your ML pipeline.

The next part of the book is about implementation and deployment and we start with how to use fastText in a Python environment in the next chapter.

Using FastText in Your Own Models 3

In this section, you will learn how to use fastText models in conjunction with other popular NLP libraries, such as Gensim and spaCy. You will also learn how to make fastText part of your pipeline, which will probably include these other tools as well.

The Chapter 5, *FastText in Python*, is about creating models in Python, either using the official Python bindings for fastText, or you can choose to use the Gensim library, which is a popular Python library for NLP.

In the Chapter 6, *Machine Learning and Deep Learning Models*, you will understand how to integrate fastText into your NLP pipeline if you have pipelines already built using either the statistical machine learning or deep learning paradigms. In the case of statistical machine learning, this chapter takes the example of the scikit-learn library, and in the case of deep learning, Keras, Tensorflow, and PyTorch are taken into account.

The Chapter 7, *Deploying Models to Mobile and Web*, is mainly about deployment and how you can integrate fastText models in live production-grade customer applications.

5
FastText in Python

The use of fastText is specifically to transform words and sentences into efficient vector representations. Although fastText is written in C++, there are community-written Python bindings to train and use the models. Along with that, Python is one of the most popular languages used for NLP, and hence there are many other popular libraries in Python that support fastText models and the training of fastText models. Gensim and Spacy are two popular libraries that make it easy to load these vectors, transform, lemmatize, and perform other NLP tasks efficiently. This chapter will focus on how to use fastText with Python and its popular libraries. This chapter will also focus on showing you some common tasks that the two libraries can do to work with fastText models.

The topics that are covered in this chapter are as follows:

- FastText official bindings
- PyBind
- Preprocessed data
- Unsupervised learning
- Supervised learning
- Gensim
- Training a fastText model
- Machine translation using Gensim

FastText official bindings

The steps to install the official bindings for Python are covered in the first chapter. In this section, we will cover how to use the official fastText Python package to train, load, and use the models.

Using the Python fastText library, you will be able to implement all the necessary features that can be done using the command line. Lets take a look at the ways to implement unsupervised and supervised learning using Python fastText.

 Note: In this chapter, we will be using Python3 and so the code examples will be in that. For users who are using Python2, please take a look at the *Appendix* for notes on the considerations that you need to bear in mind when using Python2.

PyBind

Python bindings for fastText are made using the excellent PyBind library. PyBind is a lightweight library meant to expose C++ types in Python and vice versa, making it an excellent choice for creating the Python bindings for fastText. It supports almost all the popular C++ compilers such as Clang, GCC, Visual Studio, and so on. Also, the creators of PyBind claim that the binaries that are generated are smaller.

 The Python-fastText library uses the fastText C++ API.

Preprocessing data

Although the performance of fastText is quite good on raw text, it's still advisable to preprocess the data before running the unsupervised algorithms or the classifier. Some points to be remembered are as follows:

- To train fastText, the encoding needs to be in UTF-8. PyBind does an excellent job of converting almost all text to UTF-8 if it's a string in Python3. If you are using Python2, then there is an extra technical detail that you need to take care of: you have to encode all of the string that you are using in UTF-8.
- Implementing some basic string processing and normalizing should make the model perform better.

The following is a simple function that can be used for normalizing your documents. This function is used in Python fastText notebooks:

```
def normalize(s):
    """
    Given a text, cleans and normalizes it. Feel free to add your own
```

```
stuff.
    """
    s = s.lower()
    # Replace ips
    s = re.sub(r'\d{1,3}\.\d{1,3}\.\d{1,3}\.\d{1,3}', ' _ip_ ', s)
    # Isolate punctuation
    s = re.sub(r'([\'\"\.\(\)\!\?\-\\\/\,])', r' \1 ', s)
    # Remove some special characters
    s = re.sub(r'([\;\:\|•«\n])', ' ', s)
    # Replace numbers and symbols with language
    s = s.replace('&', ' and ')
    s = s.replace('@', ' at ')
    s = s.replace('0', ' zero ')
    s = s.replace('1', ' one ')
    s = s.replace('2', ' two ')
    s = s.replace('3', ' three ')
    s = s.replace('4', ' four ')
    s = s.replace('5', ' five ')
    s = s.replace('6', ' six ')
    s = s.replace('7', ' seven ')
    s = s.replace('8', ' eight ')
    s = s.replace('9', ' nine ')
    return s
```

If you are using pandas to extract text from your dataset and clean it, you can also replace the missing text values in your dataset with an _empty_ label:

```
train = pd.read_csv('train.csv')
test = pd.read_csv('test.csv')
train['Text'] = train['Text'].fillna('_empty_')
test['Text'] = test['Text'].fillna('_empty_')
```

Unsupervised learning

The fastText command line implements two algorithms, cbow and skip-gram. Using the Python library, you should be able to train your models in both algorithms.

Training in fastText

Training in fastText is done using the train_unsupervised function. You can choose which algorithm to use from the model parameter.

Then, you can train a skipgram model using the following Python code:

```
sg_model = fastText.train_unsupervised(input='data.txt', model='skipgram')
```

This is similar to the command line:

```
./fasttext skipgram -input data.train -output model
```

Similarly, to train a `cbow` model you can use the following Python code:

```
cbow_model = fastText.train_unsupervised(input='data.txt', model='cbow')
```

The equivalent statement on the command line is:

```
./fasttext cbow -input data.train -output model
```

The difference between the Python code and the command line is that the command line will save the model in a file, while in the Python code, the model will be in memory, referenced by the variable. To save the model, you will need to pass explicit commands in your Python app, for example:

```
sg_model.save_model("sg_model.bin")
```

You should be able to pass all the other training parameters as well. The parameters, as well as the default values, are listed here:

```
sg_model = fastText.train_unsupervised(input, model='skipgram', lr=0.05,
dim=100, ws=5, epoch=5, minCount=5, minCountLabel=0, minn=3, maxn=6, neg=5,
wordNgrams=1, loss="ns", bucket=2000000, thread=12, lrUpdateRate=100,
t=1e-4, label="__label__", verbose=2, pretrainedVectors="")
```

These parameters hold the same meaning that you have seen while exploring the command line.

Evaluating the model

The lack of labels in the case of unsupervised learning makes evaluation a bit problematic as there is nothing to meaningfully compare the results of the model with. In the case of word embeddings, we have the same problem, but since this is a somewhat narrow domain, we can make some subjective claims. The fastText command line gives us the options of nearest neighbors and finding word similarities, which we can replicate in the Python library as we will see later.

Other techniques include using the syntactic and semantic performance of words based on the question—`words.txt` released by Google and the morphological similarity of rare words using the Stanford rare word database. Please keep in mind if you are creating word representations for a niche domain that these exact model evaluation techniques may not give good results, but the techniques should hold.

Word vectors

By default, the word vectors that are created are of 100 dimensions. They are saved in memory as NumPy arrays. So, you should be able to see the word vectors using the `get_word_vector` method:

```
>>> model.get_word_vector('targetword')
array([ 0.09973086,   ...   0.14613365], dtype=float32)
```

Nearest neighbor queries

Generally k nearest neighbors are used to rate differentiate between models. The vector representation of a target word is taken, the neighbors of the vectors are found and then it is seen if the neighbors are closer to its meaning. Since fastText representations are meant to be distributional, this assumption should hold true.

The fastText command line gives us a tool to get the nearest neighbors easily, but there is no easy way to find them in Python. There is a `find_nearest_neighbor` function in `util`, but it takes vectors as input. Hence, we will need to write some code to create a function that takes in words and the target model, and gives back the nearest neighbors according to the model. You can take a look at `python fastText unsupervised learning.ipynb` for the code to get the nearest neighbors:

```
>>> nn(sg_model, ['dog', 'pizza', 'hungry'], k=5)
words similar to dog:
dogs
pup
treats
puppy
dogie
########################################
words similar to pizza:
pizza;
pizza"
pizzas
"pizza
bread
########################################
words similar to hungry:
hungry";
hungrygirl
>hungry
hungry-girl
hungries
########################################
```

The output may be refined with some pre-normalization on the data.

Word similarity

There are various ways to find the similarity between words. In the case of fastText, one way of finding the similarity between words is to find the cosine distance between the words in the vector space. However, this method will probably not find the similarity between synonyms and antonyms, and other minute language constructs, but will solely give you a similarity score based on the context in which they are used. The words "water" and "cup" do not necessarily have anything that is similar between the two, but in context they are generally taken together and hence you may find the similarity score between them to be high.

In the Python library, you can write a small function to get the cosine similarity:

```
def similarity(v1, v2):
    n1 = np.linalg.norm(v1)
    n2 = np.linalg.norm(v2)
    return np.dot(v1, v2) / n1 / n2

v1 = sg_model.get_word_vector('drink')
v2 = sg_model.get_word_vector('drinks')
print(similarity(v1, v2))
```

In essence, you find the word vectors of the two target words using the `get_word_vector` method, and then find the cosine between them.

Model performance

You can find the performance of the model using the rare words dataset that was released by Stanford NLP. Using the `compute_similarity` function that is shared in the examples folder, we can change the function a little bit so that it works in a Python app. The implementation of the function can be seen in the unsupervised notebook. Download the rare words dataset, the link to which you will find in the references, unzip it, and then pass the text file as the first argument and the model as the second argument. You should be able to see how well your model has been able to evaluate the rare words:

```
>>> dataset, corr, oov = compute_similarity('data/rw/rw.txt', sg_model)
>>> print("{0:20s}: {1:2.0f}  (OOV: {2:2.0f}%)".format(dataset, corr, 0))
rw.txt               : 32  (OOV:  0%)
```

Model visualization

Visualizing how the word vectors happen in space is an effective way to understand the distributional properties of the model. Since the dimensions of the vectors are quite high, you will need a good dimensionality reduction technique so that the vectors can be shown in a two-dimensional frame.

The t-SNE is popular technique for dimensionality reduction that is well suited for the visualization of high-dimensional datasets. The idea in this case is to keep similar words as close together as possible, while maximizing the distance between dissimilar words. The unsupervised notebook shows the code for the t-SNE model. In our case, we have taken some words and plotted them in the graph:

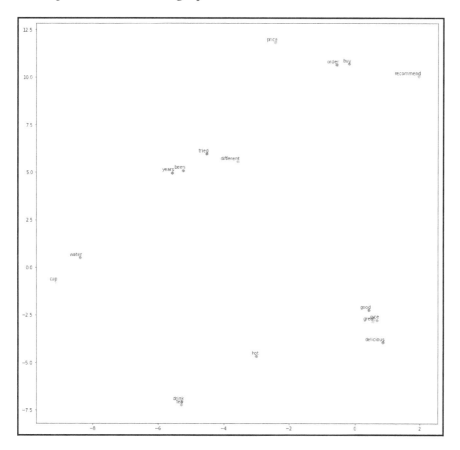

Words plotted on a graph

As you can see, "water" and "cup" are together, as they are generally used in the same context. Another two vectors that are together are "drink" and "tea." Using t-SNE to understand your model will give you a good idea of how good your model is.

Supervised learning

Similar to unsupervised learning, the fastText library provides access to the internal API for running supervised learning as well. Hence, running the fastText supervised Python API will also create the same model, which can be trained using the command line app. The advantage is that you will be able to leverage all the Python data science tools available for building an NLP classifier.

To show how to leverage the fastText classifier can be trained in Python, you can take a look at the `python fastText supervised learning.ipynb` notebook in the code. The dataset consists of reviews of fine foods from Amazon and can be downloaded from the Kaggle website, the links for which are given in the notebook.

Data preprocessing and normalization

The data preprocessing and normalization steps are similar to what you have seen in the case of unsupervised learning. In this case though, the major difference is that you will need to prefix the label with the `__label__` prefix or a label prefix of your choice. Also, it has to be saved in the fastText file in a format that is similar to the fastText command line. Since this is a classifier, you will need to actually create two files, one for training and one for model validation. One of the popular ways to split a dataset into training and testing is using the scikit-learn `train_test_split` function.

Training the model

To train the model, you will need to use the `train_supervised` method on the training file:

```
>>> su_model = fastText.train_supervised(input=train_file, epoch=25,
lr=1.0, wordNgrams=2, verbose=2, minCount=1)
```

This is similar to running this on the command line:

```
$ ./fasttext supervised -input train_file -output su_model
```

The hyperparameters are the same as what you pass in the case of supervised learning. The only difference with the unsupervised case is that the default loss function is `softmax` instead of `ns` and there is an additional `label` parameter:

```
>>> su_model = fastText.train_supervised(input=train_file, lr=0.1, dim=100,
ws=5, epoch=5, minCount=1, minCountLabel=0, minn=0, maxn=0, neg=5,
wordNgrams=1, loss="softmax", bucket=2000000, thread=12,  lrUpdateRate=100,
t=1e-4, label="__label__", verbose=2, pretrainedVectors="")
```

Similar to the case of unsupervised learning, the Python code will not save the model to a file but will save it to the variable that you defined, `su_model` in this case. This variable, `su_model`, is a Python NumPy matrix and hence we can manipulate it in standard ways.

To save the model, you will need to invoke the `save_model` method:

```
>>> su_model.save_model("su_model.bin")
```

Prediction

You can get the word vector of the word using the `get_word_vector` method, the sentence vector of a document using the `get_sentence_vector` method, and the predicted label of a model using the predict method:

```
>>> su_model.get_word_vector('restaurant')
array([ 0.9739366 , ..., -0.17078586], dtype=float32)
>>> su_model.get_sentence_vector('I love this restaurant')
array([ 0.31301185,  ... , -0.21543942], dtype=float32)
>>> su_model.predict('I love this restaurant')
(('__label__5',), array([1.00001001]))
```

You can also perform predict probabilities on your test document:

```
>>> su_model.predict("I love this restaurant", k=3)

(('__label__5', '__label__2', '__label__3'),
 array([1.00001001e+00, 1.00000034e-05, 1.00000034e-05]))
```

This is similar to this on the command line:

```
$ echo "I love this restaurant" | ./fasttext predict-prob su_model.bin - 3
__label__5 1.00001 __label__2 1e-05 __label__3 1e-05
```

Testing the model

Getting the precision and recall of your model is similar to what was seen using the command line. Similar to the command line, you will need to pass the test file and the number of labels that you need to find the precision of and recall against.

In the following example, `test_file` contains the path to the test file, and the second argument is the number of labels:

```
>>> n, p, r = su_model.test(test_file, 5)
>>> print("N\t" + str(n))
>>> print("P@{}\t{:.3f}".format(5, p))
>>> print("R@{}\t{:.3f}".format(5, r))
N 113691
P@5 0.200
R@5 1.000
```

Confusion matrix

A confusion matrix is a nice way to visualize the performance of a supervised model, specifically a classifier. It also shines when understanding which classes are performing better in a multiclass classifier. When you are creating a confusion matrix, you are essentially describing the performance of the model classifier on a test set for which the ground truth is known. Since fastText supports a classifier, you can create a confusion matrix out of it.

How to get the confusion matrix is shown in the supervised notebook. The `fasttext_confusion_matrix` function takes in a model variable, pandas test data, the label column name, and the text column name:

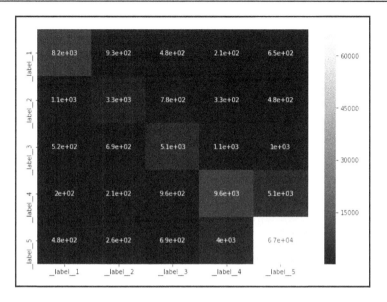

The predicted labels are shown against the true values.

Gensim

Gensim is a popular open source library for processing raw, unstructured human-generated text created by Radim Řehůřek. Some of the features that Gensim boasts are:

- Memory independence is one of the core value propositions of Gensim, which is that it should be scalable and not hold all the document in the RAM. Hence, you will be able to train documents that are significantly larger than the memory of your machine.
- Gensim has efficient implementations of various popular vector space algorithms. There has been a recent implementation of fastText in gensim as well.
- There are IO/wrappers and converters around several popular data formats as well. Remember that fastText only supports UTF-8 formats and hence Gensim might be a good choice if you have data that is in different formats.
- Different algorithms for similarity queries. So, you are not stuck with the ones that are available in fastText.

There are two ways you can use fastText through Gensim: Using the Gensim's native implementation of fastText and by using Gensim's wrapper over fastText.

Now, let's take a look at how you can use Gensim to train a fastText model.

Training a fastText model

For the example that is shown here, we will be using the Lee Corpus for training your model. To get the required data, I would recommend that you clone the Gensim repository from GitHub.

In the code examples shown here, we will be taking a look at Gensim fastText using the fake news dataset from Kaggle. First, download the data and clean the text:

```
In [1]: from gensim.models.fasttext import FastText
   ...: from gensim.corpora import Dictionary
   ...: import pandas as pd
   ...: import re
   ...: from gensim.parsing.preprocessing import remove_stopwords,
strip_punctuation
   ...: import numpy as np
   ...:

In [2]: df_fake = pd.read_csv('fake.csv')
   ...: df_fake[['title', 'text', 'language']].head()
   ...: df_fake = df_fake.loc[(pd.notnull(df_fake.text)) &
(df_fake.language == 'english')]
   ...:

In [3]: # remove stopwords and punctuations
   ...: def preprocess(row):
   ...: return strip_punctuation(remove_stopwords(row.lower()))
   ...:
   ...: df_fake['text'] = df_fake['text'].apply(preprocess)
   ...:

In [4]: # Convert data to required input format by LDA
   ...: texts = []
   ...: for line in df_fake.text:
   ...: lowered = line.lower()
   ...: words = re.findall(r'\w+', lowered)
   ...: texts.append(words)
   ...:
```

The first case we will take a look at is how to train the models using the fastText wrapper. To use the fastText wrapper, you will need to have fastText installed in your machine. You should have fastText installed if you have followed the instructions in Chapter 1, *Introducing FastText*. This wrapper is deprecated though, and the recommendation is to use the Gensim implementation of fastText:

```
>>> from gensim.models.wrappers.fasttext import FastText as FT_wrapper
```

```
>>> # Set FastText home to the path to the FastText executable
>>> ft_home = '/usr/local/bin/fasttext'

>>> # train the model
>>> model_wrapper = FT_wrapper.train(ft_home, lee_train_file)

>>> print(model_wrapper)
```

If you are interested in using the fastText implementation in Gensim, you will need to use the FastText class in `gensim.models`, which also, in addition to fastText, has word2vec and many other models that can be used:

```
In [1]:
    ...: import gensim
    ...: import os
    ...: from gensim.models.word2vec import LineSentence
    ...: from gensim.models.fasttext import FastText

In [2]: # Set file names for train and test data
    ...: data_dir = '{}'.format(os.sep).join([gensim.__path__[0], 'test',
'test_data']) + os.sep
    ...: lee_train_file = data_dir + 'lee_background.cor'
    ...: lee_data = LineSentence(lee_train_file)

In [3]: model = FastText(size=100)

In [4]: model.build_vocab(lee_data)

In [5]: # train the model
    ...: model.train(lee_data, total_examples=model.corpus_count,
epochs=model.epochs)
    ...: print(model)
FastText(vocab=1762, size=100, alpha=0.025)
```

Hyperparameters

Gensim supports the same hyperparameters that are supported in the native implementation of fastText. You should be able to set most of the hyperparameters that are there in the Facebook fastText implementation. The defaults are also mostly there already. Some differences are listed here:

- `sentences`: This can be a list of list of tokens. In general, a stream of tokens is recommended, such as `LineSentence` from the word2vec module as you have seen already. In the Facebook fastText library, this is given by the path to the file and is given by the `-input` parameter.

- `max_vocab_size`: This is to limit the RAM size. In case there are more unique words, then, this will prune the less frequent ones. This needs to be decided based on the RAM that you have. For example, if you have 2 GB memory, then the value of `max_vocab_size` is used as a parameter for that 2 GB of memory. Also, if you have not set it manually, then there is no limit set.
- `cbow_mean`: There is a difference from the fastText command here. In the original implementation for cbow, the mean of the vectors is taken. But in this case, you have the option to use the sum by passing 0 and 1 in case you want to try out the mean.
- `batch_words`: This is the target size of the batches that are passed. The default value is 10,000. This is similar to `-lrUpdateRate` in the command line, as the number of batches determines when the weights will be updated.
- `callbacks`: A list of callback functions to be executed at specific stages of the training process.
- There are no parallels for the `-supervised` and `-labels` parameters, as Gensim focuses on unsupervised learning only.

Model saving and loading

Gensim provides the save and load methods for all models, and this is implemented in the case of fastText as well:

```
In [6]: # saving a model trained via Gensim's fastText implementation
   ...: model.save('saved_model_gensim')
   ...: loaded_model = FastText.load('saved_model_gensim')
   ...: print(loaded_model)
   ...:
FastText(vocab=1762, size=100, alpha=0.025)

In [7]: import os; print(os.path.exists('saved_model_gensim'))
True
```

Loading a binary fastText model can also be achieved using the `load_fasttext_format` class method:

```
In [1]: from gensim.models.fasttext import FastText
In [2]: modelpath = "wiki.simple.bin"
In [3]: model = FastText.load_fasttext_format(modelpath)
In [4]: print(model)
FastText(vocab=111051, size=300, alpha=0.025)
```

Word vectors

In Gensim, you can check whether the words are present in the vocabulary and then get the word vectors for the words. Since fastText supports out-of-vector for the words, you should be able to get the word vectors even if the words are not present in the vocabulary. This will not work in cases where none of the character n-grams were present in the vocabulary:

```
In [1]: import gensim
   ...: import os
   ...: from gensim.models.word2vec import LineSentence
   ...: from gensim.models.fasttext import FastText
   ...:

In [2]: # Set file names for train and test data
   ...: data_dir = '{}'.format(os.sep).join([gensim.__path__[0], 'test',
'test_data']) + os.sep
   ...: lee_train_file = data_dir + 'lee_background.cor'
   ...: lee_data = LineSentence(lee_train_file)
   ...:

In [3]: model = FastText(size=100)

In [4]: # build the vocabulary
   ...: model.build_vocab(lee_data)

In [5]: # train the model
   ...: model.train(lee_data, total_examples=model.corpus_count,
epochs=model.epochs)

In [6]: print('night' in model.wv.vocab)
True

In [7]: print('nights' in model.wv.vocab) # this is not present
False

In [8]: print(model.wv['night'])
[-0.02308581 ... 0.15816787]

In [9]: print(model.wv['nights'])
[-0.02073629 ... 0.1486301 ]

In [10]: # Raises a KeyError since none of the character ngrams of the word
`axe` are present in the training data
   ...: model.wv['axe']
---------------------------------------------------------------------
KeyError Traceback (most recent call last)
<ipython-input-10-902d47f807a0> in <module>()
      1 # Raises a KeyError since none of the character ngrams of the word
```

```
`axe` are present in the training data
----> 2 model.wv['axe']

...

KeyError: 'all ngrams for word axe absent from model'
```

Model Evaluation

Since Gensim implements an unsupervised algorithm, there is no direct way of measuring how good the resulting model is. Evaluating models depends on your use case and how well it's working out in your end applications.

Gensim fastText has various methods that you can use for finding the similarity between words. The following results were received by loading the `wiki.simple.bin` model.

The easiest way to calculate the similarity between two words is using the `similarity` method:

```
In []: model.wv.similarity('night', 'nights')
Out[]: 0.9999931241743173
```

FastText computes sentence or document vectors only during supervised learning. Depending on the task, simple average word embeddings of all the normalized words in the sentence should suffice.

You can get the similarities between two documents using the `n_similarity` method. According to the Gensim documentation, this method will give the cosine similarity between the two documents. Those documents need to be passed as a list:

```
In []: model.wv.n_similarity(['sushi', 'shop'], ['japanese', 'restaurant'])
Out[]: 0.6041413398970296

In []: model.wv.n_similarity('Obama speaks to the media in
Illinois'.lower().split(), 'The president greets the press in
Chicago'.lower().spl
   ...: it())
Out[]: 0.7653119647179297
```

Gensim gives you ability to search for the most irrelevant document as well, kind of like finding the odd man out:

```
In []: model.wv.doesnt_match("breakfast cereal dinner lunch".split())
Out[]: 'cereal'
```

The `most_similar` method will give you the most similar words according to the model:

```
In []: model.wv.most_similar('food')
Out[]:
[('foods', 0.6859725713729858),
 ('foodstuffs', 0.679445743560791),
 ('seafood', 0.6695178151130676),
 ('eat', 0.5922832489013672),
 ('meals', 0.5820232629776001),
 ('meat', 0.5773770213127136),
 ('eaten', 0.5611693263053894),
 ('nutritious', 0.5602636337280273),
 ('snacks', 0.5574883818626404),
 ('cooked', 0.5470614433288574)]
=
```

Gensim provides an easy-to-use method to evaluate the model on the WordSim 353 benchmark. This dataset is a standard dataset for evaluating vector space models. There is no context around each word and the rating between the similarity of the words is on a scale of 0 to 10 in increasing order. You can find the file in `gensim/test/test_data/wordsim353.tsv` in the Gensim GitHub repository:

```
In []: model.wv.evaluate_word_pairs('wordsim353.tsv')
Out[]:
((0.6645467362164186, 2.4591009701535706e-46),
 SpearmanrResult(correlation=0.7179229895090848,
pvalue=3.58449522917263e-57),
 0.0)
```

The first result is the Pearson correlation coefficient (which is the normal correlation coefficient that we know of) and the second result is the Spearman coefficient.

You can also use the `most_similar` method to get queries of the type of *A - B + C:*

```
In []: model.wv.most_similar(positive=['story', 'dove'],
negative=['stories'])   # Vector('story') - Vector('stories') +
Vector('dove')
Out[]:
[('doves', 0.5111404657363892),
 ('dovepaw', 0.5014846324920654),
 ('turtledove', 0.4434218406677246),
 ('dovecote', 0.4430897831916809),
 ('warbler', 0.43106675148010254),
 ('warble', 0.40401384234428406),
 ('asshole', 0.4017521142959595),
 ('dovre', 0.39799436926841736),
 ('nothofagus', 0.389825701713562),
```

```
('moriarty', 0.388924241065979)]
```

Similar to this type of syntactic and semantic similarity test, if you are creating word vectors in English, you can use the `question-words.txt` task that has been prepared and released by Google. You can find the text file in `gensim/docs/notebooks/datasets/question-words.txt`.

Now, you can run the following code. Also, set the logging to info so that you can get the accuracy in terms of percentages on the different fields. There are nine types of syntactic comparisons in the dataset, family, comparative, superlative, present-participle, nationality-adjective, past-tense, and plural:

```
model.accuracy("question-words.txt")
```

This will give you an output and show you where there is a mismatch where the answers don't match with the list of words. You can evaluate based on that. If you are training for a different language, then one good investment may be to create a similar `question-words.txt` in the target language, based on different grammatical focal points in that language.

Word Mover's Distance

Word Mover's Distance (**WMD**) is a good way of capturing two documents, even when there are no common words between them. Take a look at the following example. Words like **greet** and **speaks** are fairly near to each other if we consider the WMD:

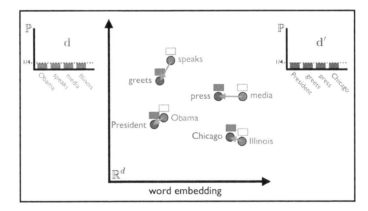

Source: `https://markroxor.github.io/gensim/static/notebooks/WMD_tutorial.html`

In Gensim, you can find the distance between two documents using the `wmdistance` method, shown as follows:

```
In []: sentence_obama = 'Obama speaks to the media in Illinois'
   ...: sentence_president = 'The president greets the press in Chicago'
   ...: sentence_obama = sentence_obama.lower().split()
   ...: sentence_president = sentence_president.lower().split()
   ...:

In []: # Remove stopwords.
   ...: stop_words = stopwords.words('english')
   ...: sentence_obama = [w for w in sentence_obama if w not in stop_words]
   ...: sentence_president = [w for w in sentence_president if w not in
stop_words]

In []: distance = model.wv.wmdistance(sentence_obama, sentence_president)
   ...: print('distance = %.4f' % distance)
distance = 4.9691
```

You can initialize a word mover similarity class on your corpus:

```
from gensim.similarities import WmdSimilarity
num_best = 10
instance = WmdSimilarity(wmd_corpus, model, num_best=10)
```

Here, `wmd_corpus` is your corpus and `model` is your trained fastText model. Now, you can run a query on the instance, which is simply a *lookup* on the class.

Getting more out of the training process

As we are going through the model training process, you will also be interested in knowing the progress and performance of the model. Understanding how the model learns can be very helpful and makes it easier to debug the model and improve it.

Another concern that may arise is training on large corpora. Training multiple epochs on large corpora may take a lot of time and hence you may want to save the model after the completion of each epoch.

In such scenarios, Gensim implements the callback parameter, which takes a sequence of subclasses of `CallbackAny2Vec` from `gensim.models.callbacks module`. Using this class, you can create classes that save the function at specific points in the training process:

```
from gensim.test.utils import common_texts as sentences
from gensim.models.callbacks import CallbackAny2Vec
from gensim.models import Word2Vec
from gensim.test.utils import get_tmpfile
```

```
class EpochSaver(CallbackAny2Vec):
    "Callback to save model after every epoch"
    def __init__(self, path_prefix):
        self.path_prefix = path_prefix
        self.epoch = 0
    def on_epoch_end(self, model):
        output_path = '{}_epoch{}.model'.format(self.path_prefix,
self.epoch)
        print("Save model to {}".format(output_path))
        model.save(output_path)
        self.epoch += 1

# to save the similarity scores
similarity = []

class EpochLogger(CallbackAny2Vec):
    "Callback to log information about training"
    def __init__(self):
        self.epoch = 0
    def on_epoch_begin(self, model):
        print("Epoch #{} start".format(self.epoch))
    def on_epoch_end(self, model):
        print("Epoch #{} end".format(self.epoch))
        self.epoch += 1
    def on_batch_begin(self, model):
        similarity.append(model.wv.similarity('woman', 'man'))
```

The `EpochSaver` class saves the model at every ending of the epoch cycle. The `EpochLogger` class does two things. It prints the epoch start and stop, and whenever there is a batch begin cycle, it saves the similarity score to a list named similarity. We will use this list later for visualization.

Now, instantiate these classes and pass them to the model training process:

```
import gensim
from gensim.models.word2vec import LineSentence
from gensim.models.fasttext import FastText

# Set file names for train and test data
lee_train_file = './gensim/gensim/test/test_data/lee_background.cor'
lee_data = LineSentence(lee_train_file)

model_gensim = FastText(size=100)

# build the vocabulary
model_gensim.build_vocab(lee_data)

# instantiate the callbacks
```

```
epoch_saver = EpochSaver(get_tmpfile("temporary_model"))
epoch_logger = EpochLogger()

# train the model
model_gensim.train(lee_data,
                   total_examples=model_gensim.corpus_count,
                   epochs=model_gensim.epochs,
                   callbacks=[epoch_saver, epoch_logger])

print(model_gensim)
```

When you run this code, you should be able to see the logger working and logging the epochs. Also, the different models will get saved onto disk.

To see how the similarity scores have progressed with the training, you can start a visdom server. Visdom is a visualization package by Facebook, which runs as a server. Its advantage is that you can send data to it, and the update parameters can be monitored using a web browser. To start a visdom server, you will need to have visdom installed and then you can run it from the command line:

```
$ pip install visdom
$ python -m visdom.server
```

Now, you can pass the similarity scores to the server:

```
import visdom
vis = visdom.Visdom()

trace = dict(x=list(range(len(similarity))), y=similarity,
mode="markers+lines", type='custom',
             marker={'color': 'red', 'symbol': 104, 'size': "10"},
             text=["one", "two", "three"], name='1st Trace')
layout = dict(title="First Plot", xaxis={'title': 'x1'}, yaxis={'title':
'x2'})

vis._send({'data': [trace], 'layout': layout, 'win': 'mywin'})
```

If you open the server at `http://localhost:8097`, you should be able to see this graph:

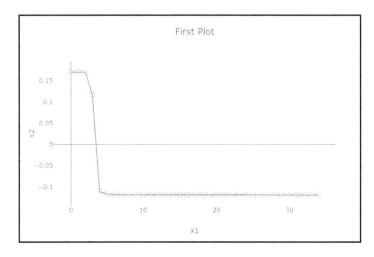

An example of a generated visdom graph

Machine translation using Gensim

According to Mikolov's 2013 paper, the link to which is given in the references, you can use the following method, which consists of two steps:

1. First, monolingual models of languages are built using large amounts of text
2. A small bilingual dictionary is used to learn a linear projection between languages

So for the first step, you can simply use the fastText models that are prebuilt and shared on the `fasttext.cc` website. In this section, we will take a look at how to implement the second step using Gensim.

The aim is to train a translation matrix, which is essentially a linear transformation matrix that links the source word vectors and the target word vectors.

You can download the transformation file from source language to target language; a good source is the Facebook muse documentation and your languages of interest may be listed there. If not, then you will need to put the effort into creating the transformation file yourself. In the example for this section, which you can find in the repo, the `en-it.txt` file was used for the English to Italian translation and it had 103,612 similar words, and hence you should probably create similar word transformation files for your models to be somewhat good in performance. Once you have the models and the transformation file, load the transformation file to a `word_pair` tuple and load the vectors to respective source target models. Once done, you can run code that looks like the following:

```
transmat = translation_matrix.TranslationMatrix(source_word_vec,
target_word_vec, word_pair)
transmat.train(word_pair)
print ("the shape of translation matrix is: ",
transmat.translation_matrix.shape)
```

At prediction time, for any given new word, we can map it to the other language space by computing $z = Wx$, and then we find the word that is closest in representation to the z vector in the target language space. The distance metric that is considered is the cosine similarity. This works similarly to the code shown here:

```
# The pair is in the form of (English, Italian), we can see whether the
translated word is correct
words = [("one", "uno"), ("two", "due"), ("three", "tre"), ("four",
"quattro"), ("five", "cinque")]
source_word, target_word = zip(*words)
translated_word = transmat.translate(source_word, 5)
for k, v in translated_word.iteritems():
    print ("word ", k, " and translated word", v)
```

You should be able to see an output that looks similar to the following code:

```
('word ', 'one', ' and translated word', [u'solo', u'due', u'tre',
u'cinque', u'quattro'])
('word ', 'two', ' and translated word', [u'due', u'tre', u'quattro',
u'cinque', u'otto'])
('word ', 'three', ' and translated word', [u'tre', u'quattro', u'due',
u'cinque', u'sette'])
('word ', 'four', ' and translated word', [u'tre', u'quattro', u'cinque',
u'due', u'sette'])
('word ', 'five', ' and translated word', [u'cinque', u'tre', u'quattro',
u'otto', u'dieci'])
```

We can see that the translations are convincing. The vectors are plotted on the following graph:

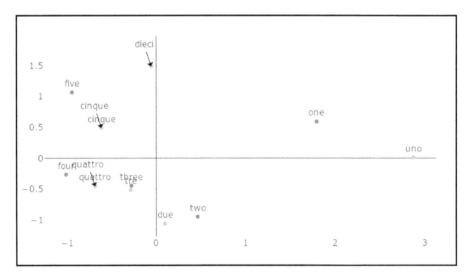

Vectors plotted on graph

Code on model training and assessing the visualizations in more detail is shown in the Jupyter notebook `gensim translation matrix with fasttext.ipynb`.

Summary

With this, we have come to the end of this chapter, where we discussed how to perform training, validation, and prediction in a Python environment. To achieve that, we focused on two packages, the official fastText Python package and the Gensim package.

In the next chapter, we will take a look at how to integrate fastText into a machine learning or a deep learning pipeline.

6
Machine Learning and Deep Learning Models

In almost all of the applications that we have been discussing up to now, the implicit assumption has been that you are creating a new machine learning NLP pipeline. Now, that may not always be the case. If you are already working on an established platform, fastText may also be a good addition to make the pipeline better.

This chapter will give you some of the methods and recipes for implementing fastText using popular frameworks such as scikit-learn, Keras, TensorFlow, and PyTorch. We will look at how we can augment the power of word embeddings in fastText, using other deep neural architectures such as **convolutional neural networks** (**CNN**) or attention networks to solve various NLP problems.

The topics covered in this chapter are as follows:

- Scikit-learn and fastText
- Embeddings
- Keras
- Embeddings layer in Keras
- Convolutional neural network architectures
- TensorFlow
- PyTorch
- Torchtext

Scikit-learn and fastText

In this section, we will be talking about how to integrate fastText into your statistical models. The most common and popular library for statistical machine learning is scikit-learn, so we will focus on that.

scikit-learn is one of the most popular machine learning tools and the reason is that the API is very simple and uniform. The flow is like this:

1. You basically convert your data into matrix format.
2. Then, you create an instance of the predictor class.
3. Using the instance, you run the `fit` method on the data.
4. Once the model is created, you can run `predict` on it.

This means that you can create a custom classifier by defining the fit and predict methods.

Custom classifiers for fastText

Since we are interested in combining fastText word vectors with the linear classifiers, you cannot pass the whole vectors and would need a way to define a single vector. In this case, let's go with the mean:

```
class MeanEmbeddingVectorizer(object):
    def __init__(self, ft_wv):
        self.ft_wv = ft_wv
        if len(ft_wv)>0:
            self.dim = ft_wv[next(iter(all_words))].shape[0]
        else:
            self.dim=0
    def fit(self, X, y):
        return self

    def transform(self, X):
        return np.array([
            np.mean([self.ft_wv[w] for w in words if w in self.ft_wv]
                    or [np.zeros(self.dim)], axis=0)
            for words in X
        ])
```

Now, you will need to pass the token dictionary to the model, which can be built from the fastText library:

```
f = load_model(FT_MODEL)

all_words = set([x for tokens in data['tokens'].values for x in tokens])

wv_dictionary = {w: f.get_word_vector(w) for w in all_words}
```

Bringing the whole thing together

You can use scikit-learn's `Pipeline` to combine the whole pipeline, demonstrated as follows:

```
etree_w2v = Pipeline([("fasttext word-vector vectorizer",
MeanEmbeddingVectorizer(wv_dictionary)),
                        ("extra trees",
ExtraTreesClassifier(n_estimators=200))])
```

The whole code is shown in the statistical machine learning notebook. For further ways of building a better model is if you can find better ways of reducing the word vectors, TF-IDF is shown in the shared notebook. Another way of reducing the word vectors is looking at the hashing transformer.

In the next sections, we will take a look at how to embed fastText vectors in deep learning models.

Embeddings

As you have seen, when you need to work with text in machine learning, you need to convert the text into numerical values. The logic is the same in neural architectures as well. In neural networks, you implement this using the embeddings layer. All modern deep learning libraries provide an embeddings API for use.

The embeddings layer is a useful and versatile layer used for various purposes:

- It can be used to learn word embeddings to be used in an application later
- It can be used with a larger model where the embeddings are also tuned as part of the model
- It can be used to load a pretrained word embedding

It is in the third point that will be the focus of this section. The idea is to utilize fastText to create superior embeddings, which can then be injected into your model using this embedding layer. Normally the embeddings layer is initialized with random weights, but in this case we will be injecting it with the word embeddings from our fastText model.

Keras

Keras is a widely popular high-level neural network API. It supports TensorFlow, CNTK, and Theano as the backend. Due to the user-friendly API of Keras, many people use it in lieu of the base libraries.

Embedding layer in Keras

The embedding layer will be the first hidden layer of the Keras network and you will need to specify three arguments: input dimension, output dimension, and input length. Since we will be using fastText to make our model better, we will also need to pass the weights parameter with the embedding matrix and make the trainable matrix to be false:

```
embedding_layer = Embedding(num_words,
                            EMBEDDING_DIM,
                            weights=[embedding_matrix],
                            input_length=MAX_SEQUENCE_LENGTH,
                            trainable=False)
```

Another thing that we need to take care of is that we need to map words to integers and integers to words. In Keras, you do this using the `Tokenizer` class.

Let's look at this in action as part of a CNN.

Convolutional neural networks

When we talk in terms of mixing word embeddings and neural networks, convolutional networks are something that have yielded good results. CNNs are created by applying several layers of convolutions with nonlinear activation functions such as ReLu or *tanh* applied to the results.

Lets talk a little bit about what a convolution means. A convolution of any function with respect to another function is the integral that expresses the amount of overlap of one function as it is passed over the other function. You can think of this as blending one function into another. In signal theory, this is how experts understand convolutions: the output signal is a convolution of the input signal with the impulse response of the environment. The impulse response of any environment essentially identifies and distinguishes the environment.

In a traditional feedforward network, we connect each input neuron to each output neuron in the next layer. In CNNs, we instead use convolutions on the input to compute the output. During the training phase, a CNN will automatically learn the values of the filters.

CNNs are generally used with word embeddings, and it is here that fastText comes into the picture and has the potential to bring huge gains in terms of classification accuracy by providing better word representations. The architecture is thus composed of three key sections:

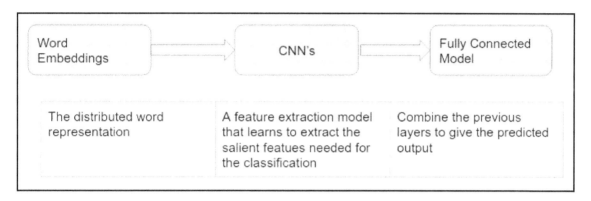

If you have these three pieces of the architecture already in place in your classification pipeline, you can identify the word embeddings part and see whether changing that to fasttext gives you an improvement in terms of the predictions.

In this example, we will be taking a look at the previous example of Yelp reviews and trying to classify them using a convolution neural network. For the sake of brevity, we will fit a pretrained dataset that has been released, but you will probably be working on a domain-specific use case and hence you should be integrating the creation of the model, as shown in the previous chapter. As you have seen, you can use fastText library or the Gensim library.

From a high level, the steps are as follows:

1. Text samples in the dataset are converted into sequences of word indices. A *word index* would simply be an integer ID for the word. We will only consider the top 20,000 most common words in the dataset, and we will truncate the sequences to a maximum of 1,000 words. This is done for ease of computation. You can play around with this approach and find the approach that brings the greatest generalization.
2. Prepare an embedding matrix, which will contain at index i the embedding vector for the word i in the word index.

3. The embedding matrix is then loaded to the Keras embedding layer, and will set the layer to be frozen so that it is not updated while training.

4. The layers that come after it will be the convolution networks. At the end, there will be a softmax layer to converge the output to our five categories.

In this case, we can use the pandas library to create the list of input text and the list of the output labels:

```
>>> df = pd.read_csv('yelp_review.csv')
>>> texts = df.text.values
>>> labels = df.stars.values
>>> texts = texts[:20000]
>>> labels = labels[:20000]
>>> print('Found %s texts.' % len(texts))
Found 20000 texts.
```

Now, we will need to format our text samples and labels into tensors that can be fed into the neural network. This is the place where we will be using the `Tokenizer` class. We will also need to pad the sequences as we need matrices of equal lengths:

```
>>> # finally, vectorize the text samples into a 2D integer tensor
>>> tokenizer = Tokenizer(num_words=MAX_NUM_WORDS)
>>> tokenizer.fit_on_texts(texts)
>>> sequences = tokenizer.texts_to_sequences(texts)
>>> word_index = tokenizer.word_index
>>> print('Found %s unique tokens.' % len(word_index))
Found 45611 unique tokens.
>>> data = pad_sequences(sequences, maxlen=MAX_SEQUENCE_LENGTH)
>>> labels = to_categorical(np.asarray(labels))
>>> print('Shape of data tensor:', data.shape)
>>> print('Shape of label tensor:', labels.shape)
Shape of data tensor: (20000, 1000)
Shape of label tensor: (20000, 6)
>>> # split the data into a training set and a validation set
>>> indices = np.arange(data.shape[0])
>>> np.random.shuffle(indices)
>>> data = data[indices]
>>> labels = labels[indices]
>>> num_validation_samples = int(VALIDATION_SPLIT * data.shape[0])
>>> x_train = data[:-num_validation_samples]
>>> y_train = labels[:-num_validation_samples]
>>> x_val = data[-num_validation_samples:]
>>> y_val = labels[-num_validation_samples:]
```

Now we will be using our fastText embeddings. In this case, we are using pretrained embeddings, but you can train your own embeddings on the fly during the training process. You have the choice of loading from the `.vec` file, but since this is fastText, we will load from the BIN file. The advantage of using the BIN file is that the out of vocabulary case will be avoided to a large extent. We will use the fastText model and generate an embedding matrix:

```
>>> print('Preparing embedding matrix.')

>>># load the fasttext model
>>> f = load_model(FT_MODEL)

>>> # prepare embedding matrix
>>> num_words = min(MAX_NUM_WORDS, len(word_index) + 1)
>>> embedding_matrix = np.zeros((num_words, EMBEDDING_DIM))
>>> for word, i in word_index.items():
...     if i >= MAX_NUM_WORDS:
...         continue
...     embedding_vector = f.get_word_vector(word)
...     if embedding_vector is not None:
...         # words not found in embedding index will be all-zeros.
...         embedding_matrix[i] = embedding_vector
```

We load this to the embedding layer. It is important to note that the trainable parameter should be set to `False` to prevent the weights from being updated, as follows:

```
>>> # load pre-trained word embeddings into an Embedding layer
>>> embedding_layer = Embedding(num_words,
...                             EMBEDDING_DIM,
...                             weights=[embedding_matrix],
...                             input_length=MAX_SEQUENCE_LENGTH,
...                             trainable=False)
```

Now, we can build a 1D ConvNet to apply to our Yelp classification problem:

```
>>> # train a 1D convnet with global maxpooling
>>> sequence_input = Input(shape=(MAX_SEQUENCE_LENGTH,), dtype='int32')
>>> embedded_sequences = embedding_layer(sequence_input)
>>> x = Conv1D(128, 5, activation='relu')(embedded_sequences)
>>> x = MaxPooling1D(5)(x)
>>> x = Conv1D(128, 5, activation='relu')(x)
>>> x = MaxPooling1D(5)(x)
>>> x = Conv1D(128, 5, activation='relu')(x)
>>> x = GlobalMaxPooling1D()(x)
>>> x = Dense(128, activation='relu')(x)
>>> preds = Dense(6, activation='softmax')(x)
```

The summary of this model is shown as follows:

```
Layer (type) Output Shape Param #
=================================================================
input_1 (InputLayer) (None, 1000) 0
_____
embedding_1 (Embedding) (None, 1000, 300) 6000000
_____
conv1d_1 (Conv1D) (None, 996, 128) 192128
_____
max_pooling1d_1 (MaxPooling1 (None, 199, 128) 0
_____
conv1d_2 (Conv1D) (None, 195, 128) 82048
_____
max_pooling1d_2 (MaxPooling1 (None, 39, 128) 0
_____
conv1d_3 (Conv1D) (None, 35, 128) 82048
_____
global_max_pooling1d_1 (Glob (None, 128) 0
_____
dense_1 (Dense) (None, 128) 16512
_____
dense_2 (Dense) (None, 6) 774
=================================================================
Total params: 6,373,510
Trainable params: 373,510
Non-trainable params: 6,000,000
_____
```

Now, you can try out some other hyperparameters and try to improve the accuracy from here.

In this section, you saw how to use the fastText word embeddings as part of a larger CNN Keras classifier. Using a similar approach, you can use fastText embeddings with whichever neural architectures benefit from word embeddings in Keras.

TensorFlow

TensorFlow is a computation library developed by Google. It is quite popular now and is used by many companies to create their neural network models. After what you have seen in Keras, the logic behind augmenting TensorFlow models using fastText is the same.

Word embeddings in TensorFlow

To create word embeddings in TensorFlow, you will need to create an embeddings matrix where all the tokens in your list of documents have unique IDs, and so each document is a vector of these IDs. Now, let's say you have an embedding in a NumPy array called `word_embedding`, with `vocab_size` rows and `embedding_dim` columns, and you want to create a tensor `W`. Taking a specific example, the sentence "I have a cat." can be split up into ["I", "have", "a", "cat", "."], and the tensor of the corresponding `word_ids` will be of shape 5. To map these word IDs into vectors, create the word embedding variable and use the `tf.nn.embedding_lookup` function:

```
word_embeddings = tf.get_variable("word_embeddings",
                            [vocabulary_size, embedding_size])
embedded_word_ids = tf.nn.embedding_lookup(word_embeddings, word_ids)
```

After this, the `embedded_word_ids` tensor will have shape `[5, embedding_size]` in our example and contain the embeddings (dense vectors) for each of the five words.

To be able to use a word embedding with pretrained vectors, create `W` as a `tf.Variable` and initialize it from the NumPy array via a `tf.placeholder()`:

```
with tf.name_scope("embedding"):
    W = tf.Variable(tf.constant(0.0,
                            shape=[doc_vocab_size,
                                embedding_dim]),
                        trainable=False,
                        name="W")
  embedding_placeholder = tf.placeholder(tf.float32,
      [doc_vocab_size, embedding_dim])
  embedding_init = W.assign(embedding_placeholder)
  embedded_chars = tf.nn.embedding_lookup(W, x)
```

You can then pass the actual embeddings in the TensorFlow session:

```
sess = tf.Session()
sess.run(embedding_init, feed_dict={embedding_placeholder: embedding})
```

This will avoid storing a copy of the embeddings in the graph, but it does require enough memory to keep two copies of the matrix at once (one for the NumPy array and one for the `tf.Variable`). You would want to have word embeddings constant during the training process, so as discussed earlier, the trainable parameter for the embeddings needs to be `False`.

RNN architectures

NLP has always been considered to be an excellent use case for LSTMs and RNN-type neural architectures. LSTMs and RNNs use sequential processing. NLP has always been considered one of the biggest use cases because the meaning of any sentence is context-based. The meaning of a word can be considered to have meaning based on all the words that came before it:

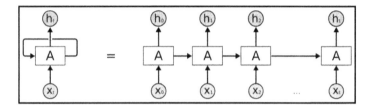

Now, when you are running an LSTM network, you need to convert the words into an embedding layer. Generally in such cases, a random initializer is used. But, you probably should be able to increase the performance of the model using a fastText model. Let's take a look at how a fastText model is used in such cases.

In this example, the crawl vectors that are released by Facebook are loaded into memory. In your use case, you should probably train a fastText model on your text corpus and load that model. We are creating the embedding using the VEC file here, but you can chose to load from a `.bin` file as well, as shown in the Keras example:

```
#Load fasttext vectors
filepath_glove = 'crawl-300d-2M.vec'
glove_vocab = []
glove_embd=[]
embedding_dict = {}

with open(filepath_glove) as file:
    for index, line in enumerate(file):
        values = line.strip().split() # Word and weights separated by space
        if index == 0:
            glove_vocab_size = int(values[0])
            embedding_dim = int(values[1])
        else:
            row = line.strip().split(' ')
            vocab_word = row[0]
            glove_vocab.append(vocab_word)
            embed_vector = [float(i) for i in row[1:]] # convert to list of
float
            embedding_dict[vocab_word]=embed_vector
```

Call the block of text that is your target of interest, and then run the normal cleaning step. Similar to the example in Keras, you will next need a mechanism that maps the tokens to a unique integer and a way to get the token back from the integer. So, we will need to create a dictionary and a reverse dictionary with the words:

```
#Create dictionary and reverse dictionary with word ids

def build_dictionaries(words):
    count = collections.Counter(words).most_common() #creates list of
word/count pairs;
    dictionary = dict()
    for word, _ in count:
        dictionary[word] = len(dictionary) #len(dictionary) increases each
iteration
        reverse_dictionary = dict(zip(dictionary.values(),
dictionary.keys()))
    return dictionary, reverse_dictionary

dictionary, reverse_dictionary = build_dictionaries(training_data)
```

We create the embedding array from the dictionary that we created using the fastText model:

```
#Create embedding array

doc_vocab_size = len(dictionary)
dict_as_list = sorted(dictionary.items(), key = lambda x : x[1])

embeddings_tmp=[]

for i in range(doc_vocab_size):
    item = dict_as_list[i][0]
    if item in glove_vocab:
        embeddings_tmp.append(embedding_dict[item])
    else:
        rand_num = np.random.uniform(low=-0.2, high=0.2,size=embedding_dim)
        embeddings_tmp.append(rand_num)

# final embedding array corresponds to dictionary of words in the document
embedding = np.asarray(embeddings_tmp)

# create tree so that we can later search for closest vector to prediction
tree = spatial.KDTree(embedding)
```

Next, we set up the RNN model. We will be reading three words at a time and hence our x is a matrix with an undetermined number of rows and three columns wide. Another input of note is the `embedding_placeholder` has one row per word and has a width of 300 dimensions, corresponding to the number of dimensions for the input word vector.

Then, the TensorFlow `tf.nn.embedding_lookup()` function can be used to look up each of our inputs from x in matrix W, resulting in the 3D tensor `embedded_chars`. This can then be fed into the RNN:

```
# create input placeholders
x = tf.placeholder(tf.int32, [None, n_input])
y = tf.placeholder(tf.float32, [None, embedding_dim])

# RNN output node weights and biases
weights = { 'out': tf.Variable(tf.random_normal([n_hidden, embedding_dim]))
}
biases = { 'out': tf.Variable(tf.random_normal([embedding_dim])) }

with tf.name_scope("embedding"):
    W = tf.Variable(tf.constant(0.0, shape=[doc_vocab_size,
embedding_dim]), trainable=False, name="W")
    embedding_placeholder = tf.placeholder(tf.float32, [doc_vocab_size,
embedding_dim])
    embedding_init = W.assign(embedding_placeholder)
    embedded_chars = tf.nn.embedding_lookup(W,x)
# reshape input data
x_unstack = tf.unstack(embedded_chars, n_input, 1)

# create RNN cells
rnn_cell =
rnn.MultiRNNCell([rnn.BasicLSTMCell(n_hidden),rnn.BasicLSTMCell(n_hidden)])
outputs, states = rnn.static_rnn(rnn_cell, x_unstack, dtype=tf.float32)

# capture only the last output
pred = tf.matmul(outputs[-1], weights['out']) + biases['out']
```

Now that we have the RNN, we need to figure out how to train it and what kind of cost function can be used. FastText internally uses the softmax function. The softmax function may not be suitable as a cost function in this case because, by definition, softmax normalizes the vectors before comparing. Thus, the actual vector may grow or shrink in an arbitrary manner. There may be a good case for having the final vectors with the same magnitude as the vectors in the training set, and thus with the same magnitudes as the pretrained vectors. In this example, the focus is on L2 loss:

```
cost = tf.reduce_mean(tf.nn.l2_loss(pred-y))
optimizer =
tf.train.AdamOptimizer(learning_rate=learning_rate).minimize(cost)
```

Only the important bit of the code snippet is shown here. You will find the whole code in the TensorFlow notebook in the `chapter6` folder: `https://github.com/PacktPublishing/Learn-fastText/blob/master/chapter6/TensorFlow%20rnn.ipynb`.

PyTorch

Following the same logic as the previous two libraries, you can use the `torch.nn.EmbeddingBag` class to inject the pretrained embeddings. There is a small drawback though. Keras and TensorFlow make the assumption that your tensors are actually implemented as NumPy arrays, while in the case of PyTorch, that's not the case. PyTorch implements the torch tensor. Generally, this is not an issue, but this means that you will need to write your own text conversion and tokenizing pipelines. To circumvent all this rewriting and reinvention of the wheel, you can use the torchtext library.

The torchtext library

The torchtext is an excellent library that takes care of most of the preprocessing steps that you need to build your NLP model. Basically, think of torchtext as something that acts like *configuration as code* in a loose sense of the term. So, it makes sense to understand the torchtext data paradigm, which takes around three hours, instead of writing custom code, which will probably seem easier but would involve countless hours of confusion and debugging. And to top it off, it can build prebuilt models, including fastText.

Now, let's take a look at how that is done.

Data classes in torchtext

We will first call all the required libraries. Take note that you are calling data that contains the required data classes for our use:

```
from torchtext import data
import spacy
...
```

We will use `spacy` for the tokenization step, for which torchtext has excellent support. torchtext provides excellent support for calling and loading fastText libraries:

```
from torchtext.vocab import FastText
vectors = FastText('simple')
```

This will download the `wiki.simple.bin` model. If you provide the name `en`, it will download and load `wiki.en.bin`. If you load `fr`, then it will load `wiki.fr.bin`, and so on.

You will probably be loading the data from a CSV or from a text file. In that case, you will need to open the file, possibly in pandas, extract the relevant fields, and then save them in a separate file. torchtext is not able to distinguish between training and validation, and hence you will probably need to separate out those files as well:

```
def clean_str(string):
    string = re.sub(r"[^A-Za-z0-9(),!?\'\`]", " ", string)
    string = re.sub(r"\'s", " \'s", string)
    string = re.sub(r"\'ve", " \'ve", string)
    string = re.sub(r"n\'t", " n\'t", string)
    string = re.sub(r"\'re", " \'re", string)
    string = re.sub(r"\'d", " \'d", string)
    string = re.sub(r"\'ll", " \'ll", string)
    string = re.sub(r",", " , ", string)
    string = re.sub(r"!", " ! ", string)
    string = re.sub(r"\(", " \( ", string)
    string = re.sub(r"\)", " \) ", string)
    string = re.sub(r"\?", " \? ", string)
    string = re.sub(r"\s{2,}", " ", string)
    return string.strip().lower()

def prepare_csv(df, seed=999):
    df['text'] = df['text'].apply(clean_str)
    df_train, df_test = train_test_split(df, test_size=0.2)
    df_train.to_csv("yelp_tmp/dataset_train.csv", index=False)
    df_test.to_csv("yelp_tmp/dataset_val.csv", index=False)
```

You will now need to define the data and build the vocabulary. You can do this using the data module. This module has the data classes to define the pipelining steps and run the batching, padding, and numericalization. First, you will need to define the type of fields using data.Fields. This class defines the common datatypes that can be used to create the required tensor. You can also define some common instructions to define how the tensor should be created. Once the fields are created, you can call TabularDataset to create the dataset using the instructions defined in the field. The common instructions are passed as parameters:

```
# Define all the types of fields
# pip install spacy for the tokenizer to work (or remove to use default)
TEXT = data.Field(lower=True, include_lengths=True, fix_length=150,
tokenize='spacy')
LABEL = data.Field(sequential=True, use_vocab=False)

# we use the index field to re-sort test data after processing
INDEX = data.Field(sequential=False)

train_fields=[
    (text_label, TEXT),
    (stars_label, LABEL)
]

train_fields=[
    (text_label, TEXT),
    (stars_label, LABEL)
]

train = data.TabularDataset(
    path='yelp_tmp/dataset_train.csv', format='csv', skip_header=True,
    fields=train_fields)

test_fields=[
    (id_label, INDEX),
    (text_label, TEXT),
    (stars_label, LABEL)
]
test = data.TabularDataset(
        path='yelp_tmp/dataset_val.csv', format='csv', skip_header=True,
        fields=test_fields)
```

- sequential=True means that the column has sequences. We probably want that to be the case for labels as the example is pretty much a comparison, but in cases where that is not the case, set this to false.

- We are specifying the tokenizer to be spacy in this case, but you can specify custom functions.
- `fix_length` pads or trims all sequences to fixed lengths of 150 in this case.
- `lower` specifies we are setting all English letters to lowercase.

Once the datasets are created, you will need to create the vocabulary so that we can convert the tokens into integer numbers later. It is here that we are going to build the vocabulary from the fastText vectors that we loaded earlier:

```
max_size = 30000
TEXT.build_vocab(train, test, vectors=vectors, max_size=max_size)
INDEX.build_vocab(test)
```

Using the iterators

You can now use an iterator to iterate over the dataset. In this case, we are using `BucketIterator`, which has the additional advantage that it batches examples of similar lengths together. This reduces the amount of padding needed:

```
train = data.BucketIterator(train, batch_size=32,
                            sort_key=lambda x: len(x.text),
                            sort_within_batch=True, repeat=False)
test = data.BucketIterator(test, batch_size=128,
                           sort_key=lambda x: len(x.text),
                           sort_within_batch=True, train=False,
                           repeat=False)
```

So, you will be able to run simple `for` loops on these iterators and they will provide inputs based on batches.

Bringing it all together

Finally, once all these steps are done, you can initialize your PyTorch model, and you will need to set the pretrained vectors as the weights of the model. In the example, an RNN model was created and the word vectors were initialized from the earlier field vectors. This will take care of handling the `lookup_table` in PyTorch:

```
model = RNNModel('GRU', ntokens, emsize, nhidden, 6,
                 nlayers, dropemb=dropemb, droprnn=droprnn,
                 bidirectional=True)
model.encoder.weight.data.copy_(TEXT.vocab.vectors)
```

The code shown here includes only the things that should be new to you. For the full code, take a look at the `pytorch torchtext rnn.ipynb` notebook in the repository.

Summary

In this chapter, we took a look at how to integrate fastText word vectors into either linear machine learning models or deep learning models created in Keras, TensorFlow, and PyTorch. You also saw how word vectors can be easily assimilated into existing neural architectures that you might be using in your business application. If you are initializing the embeddings from random values, I would highly recommend that you try to initialize them using fastText values, and then see whether there are performance improvements in your model.

Deploying Models to Web and Mobile

7

For companies that depend on machine learning, it is very important to deploy their models in a scalable fashion. The models should work in the same manner that they were working in when the model was created. Deploying fastText models, both supervised and unsupervised, can be done in a variety of ways. The choice of methodology would depend on your individual needs.

In this chapter, we will focus on how to deploy fastText models in web and mobile scenarios. The topics are the following:

- Deploying to the web
- Flask
- FastText functions
- Flask endpoints
- Deploying to smaller devices
- Prerequisites – Completing the Google tutorial
- App considerations
- Adding the fastText model
- FastText in Java
- Adding library dependencies to Android
- Using library dependencies in Android
- Finally, the app

Deploying to the web

Now that you have the ways and means to create your own fastText models, you will probably need to deploy them to production so that those models can be utilized to create applications and endpoints to use. There are a lot of frameworks in Python that can be used to create such web apps. Flask, Django, and Pyramid are some popular Python web frameworks. In this section, we will take the example of flask and build a simple web nearest neighbor search application in flask.

Flask

Flask is a popular web framework, and it is classified as a microframework as it does not require any external tools or libraries. There are no database abstraction layers, or form validation, or other components built into flask. The advantage of this is that you can build a simple web app in flask with minimal lines of code. This helps fast prototyping and helps you to focus on the application code itself.

For code that is discussed in this section, take a look at the `chapter 7` folder in the repository. You will find two files, `ft_server.py` and `ft_utils.py`. The `ft_utils.py` module has the code related to the fastText server, and `ft_server.py` has the code related to the flask endpoints.

The fastText functions

If you take a look at the code, we are loading the fastText module from the `FT_MODEL` environment variable. This model is loaded as a global variable so that it can be utilized in the functions as well. Another advantage is that when the flask app is initialized, the model will also be loaded into memory. Loading the model into memory is computationally expensive and hence if we defer that operation to the initialization phase, that will improve the response timings:

```
print('loading the model')
FT_MODEL = os.environ.get('FT_MODEL')
if not FT_MODEL:
    raise ValueError('No fasttext model has been linked.')
FT_MODEL = fastText.load_model(FT_MODEL)
print('model is loaded')
```

Now, we will also get the most common words in the vocabulary, based on a threshold, and keep it in memory. We will keep the word vectors, again as a global variable, so that the computation of the word vectors is done during the initiation of the app, similar to before:

```
# Gets words with associated frequency sorted by default by descending
order
words, freq = FT_MODEL.get_words(include_freq=True)
words = words[:threshold]
vectors = np.zeros((len(words), FT_MODEL.get_dimension()), dtype=float)
for i in range(len(words)):
    wv = FT_MODEL.get_word_vector(words[i])
    wv = wv / np.linalg.norm(wv)
    vectors[i] = wv

# For efficiency preallocate the memory to calculate cosine similarities
cossims = np.zeros(len(words), dtype=float)
```

The next two functions are basically how to get the nearest words, based on the distances between the word vector for the question word and the word vectors of the other words as well. These functions have also been discussed in Chapter 5, *FastText in Python* as well.

You should be able to run the module by itself. Also, notice the time required to run the whole module.

Running the whole code takes around 10 seconds on my laptop.

The flask endpoints

For reasons of brevity, there is only one endpoint that is discussed in this app. Basically, it is used to take the incoming question word, get the answers from the nn function defined in the ft_utils.py file, and then serve the answers in JSON format:

```
@app.route('/nn/<question_word>')
def nearest_neighbours(question_word):
    answers = [a for a in nn(FT_MODEL, question_word, k=5)]
    return jsonify(dict(question=question_word, answers=answers))
```

Now, run the app in development mode and so that you can debug it:

```
$ export FLASK_APP=ft_server.py
$ export FLASK_ENV=development
$ export FT_MODEL=wiki.simple.bin
$ flask run
```

Open a new terminal and send a curl request; you should be able to see the response in the Terminal. You can see that the response is also fast:

```
$ time curl http://127.0.0.1:5000/nn/dog
{
    "answers": [
        "dogs",
        "catdog",
        "sheepdog",
        "sheepdogs",
        "breed"
    ],
    "question": "dog"
}
$ curl http://127.0.0.1:5000/nn/dog 0.01s user 0.00s system 9% cpu 0.105
total
```

We are able to have very fast responses as part of the Flask app as we tried to shift the computationally expensive portions of the code to the app initiation phase as much as possible. This is generally a good idea. As part of the web app, only do what is absolutely necessary and keep the amount of computation as part of serving the request to the minimum. This will ensure that you are building effective and useful web apps to for deploying fastText models and machine learning apps in general.

Deploying to smaller devices

As you saw in `Chapter 2`, *Creating Models Using FastText Command Line*, you can create a compressed fastText model from a whole model using a command similar to this one:

```
$ ./fasttext quantize -output <model prefix> -input <training file> -qnorm
-retrain -epoch <number of epochs> -cutoff <number of words to consider>
```

In `Chapter 4`, *Sentence Classification in FastText*, we also revisited the concept of having compressed models and how compression was achieved without much loss in performance.

This enables you to deploy machines in smaller devices as well. One of the first things that comes to mind is whether the files can be packaged with an Android app and deployed in an Android application.

In this section, I will put into place all the requirements and dependencies that should enable you to deploy an Android fastText application.

Prerequisites – Completing the Google tutorial

One of the best examples to consider is the example Android app in the Google tutorial. In case you are new to Android, go to `https://developer.android.com/training/basics/firstapp/` and complete the tutorial there. We will not go into the details here, so in summary, the steps are:

1. Install Android Studio
2. Create some simple user interfaces
3. Create the activities and define the intents
4. Build and create the APK files

For our app, we will be working along similar lines. The name of the project in our case is `Fasttext application`. So, download the latest Android Studio and fire it up:

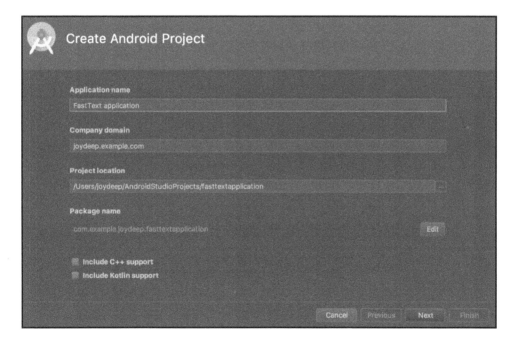

Keep on clicking **Next**, select empty activity, and click **Finish**. You should be taken to a new project window, which has a lot of boilerplate code for Android already done for you. Now, open up the Google tutorial and follow all the steps in the tutorial. If you are already an experienced Android developer, then you can open the project from the GitHub repository. First, do a `git fetch` and check out the `android_starting` branch:

```
git fetch
git checkout android_starting
```

Now, if you compile the app and create an APK, you should be able to get the following screen. Or if you have ADB set up, you can just select **Run** and see the app in your emulator.

To build an APK, you can click the **Build APK(s)** button in your Android Studio:

Please go through the steps written in **Build a simple User interface** in the Google Android tutorial so that you finally get a simple app running, similar to this one:

Now, go through the **Start another activity** tutorial and complete the creation of another activity. The aim of this tutorial is so that you can have a separate activity triggered from the first activity:

 =>

App considerations

Now that you have two activities, you might have guessed the aim of our fastText application. We will input our text label in the first activity, and it should give us the labels in the second activity.

To achieve that, you will need to do two things:

1. Add a prebuilt fastText model to the Android app
2. Add a library that will parse the fastText model and give us the predictions

There are some points that I would like to mention here. We are going to use the fastText FTZ models here. You can argue as we had seen, fastText models are built using product quantization using methods such as nearest neighbor centroid estimations, pruning of vocabularies and hashing. This results in loss of information, although it is argued that there is no significant loss in performance. But if you are not convinced, you have the option of creating the web app as discussed in the previous section and accessing the results from your Android app, which means having the Android app as a view-only, and deferring all the computation to the server. That is a fair course to take, but is more of an engineering challenge and not within the scope of this book. In this section, we are more interested in finding out whether we can leverage the capabilities of fastText to create really small models, deploy them in mobile devices, and use them in our applications.

Now before we go ahead, build the APK and take note of the present size of the application, since size is an important matter for users if you want users to download and use the application. You probably don't want your users to uninstall the application because the memory is full, or the user is in a place where the internet is really slow and it will take a long time to download the application. So, keep the application size always in mind when designing applications for smaller devices.

Right now, the build is taking up only 1.5 MB of memory:

```
$ du -sh app-debug.apk
1.6M app-debug.apk
```

Adding the fastText model

Moving ahead, now you will need to add a fastText model to the application. Android has an asset management system which can be used for this.

First of all, download or create an FTZ model. I downloaded the `dbpedia.ftz` file from the supervised models section of the fastText website. The file is around 1.6 MB in size and hence should not bump up the APK size in the final build.

Android has a resource management system and you can use that for this purpose. Create an assets folder under the main folder and copy/paste your FTZ file there:

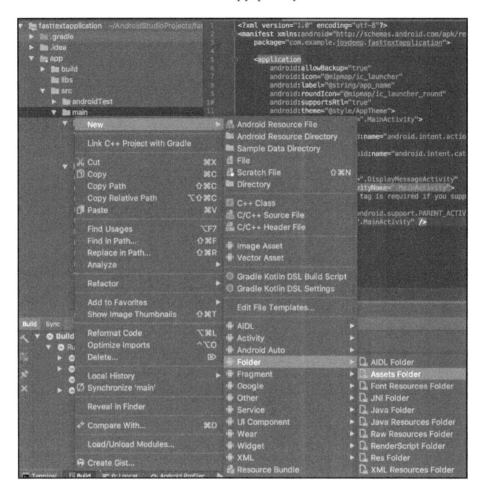

You should be able to see the file, as shown here:

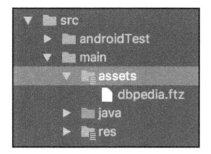

Once done, add the code to access the file using the resource manager. Since we are making the predictions in the second activity, let's access this file in the `DisplayMessageActivity.java` file.

In the `onCreate` method, create an `AssetManager` instance to access the asset files, and create an `InputStream` instance so that the file can be converted to a stream. The data will be read and manipulated from this stream, shown as follows:

```java
public class DisplayMessageActivity extends AppCompatActivity {

    @Override
    protected void onCreate(Bundle savedInstanceState) {
        super.onCreate(savedInstanceState);
        setContentView(R.layout.activity_display_message);

        // Get the Intent that started this activity and extract the string
        Intent intent = getIntent();
        String message = intent.getStringExtra(MainActivity.EXTRA_MESSAGE);

        // Get the assets from the asset manager.
        AssetManager assetManager = getAssets();
        InputStream inputStream = null;
        try {
            inputStream = assetManager.open("dbpedia.ftz");
        } catch (IOException e) {
            e.printStackTrace();
        }

        // Capture the layout's TextView and set the string as its text
        TextView textView = findViewById(R.id.textView);
        textView.setText(message);

    }
```

Press *Alt + Enter* (or *Option + Enter* on a Mac) to import missing classes. Your imports should end up as the following:

```
import android.content.Intent;
import android.content.res.AssetManager;
import android.support.v7.app.AppCompatActivity;
import android.os.Bundle;
import android.widget.TextView;

import java.io.IOException;
import java.io.InputStream;
```

FastText in Java

Now that you have the fastText model deployed in the Android app, you will need a way to access the file and serve the predictions. One way that you can do this is that you can write Java custom code using the fastText GitHub repository as a reference. The advantage of this approach is that you have more control over the code, and that might be the only option if you are writing an enterprise application, since the code of fastText is given under the BSD license. Another option is to take the fastText code and compile the code as part of the Android library, but there are a lot of issues with serving native code and it may not work on all devices. The best approach for me when adding external dependencies is if you can find core Java libraries that do the work for you.

Fortunately in this case, we have one that fits the bill. `fastText4j` is an excellent Java library by `linkfluence` on GitHub that has all the code in Java and is able to load and parse Java libraries as well. Apart from the ability to read bin and FTZ files, we also have the ability read and create Java memory mapped files, although we will not be using it here. Use the following repository to clone the repository that is a clone of the original `linkfluence` one:

```
$ git clone https://github.com/infinite-Joy/fastText4j.git
$ cd fastText4j
$ mvn clean
```

Also compile the package to an app as we will need that for testing and compilation purposes. Unzip the file that is created as a result:

```
$ mvn install -Papp
$ unzip app/fasttext4j-app.zip
$ cp target/fasttext4j-0.2.1-SNAPSHOT.jar lib/fasttext4j-0.2.1-SNAPSHOT.jar
```

This should copy a `lib/` folder and `fasttext-mmap.sh` file to your present directory. The last copy stage is not really necessary now, but this is just to show you this step is needed when you make changes to this repository and recompile the JAR again. For now, the file will have a slightly different command line. Change the `main` method in `src/main/java/fasttext/FastText.java`:

```
public static void main(String[] args) throws Exception {

    Options options = new Options();

    Option input = new Option("i", "input", true, "input model path");
    input.setRequired(true);
    options.addOption(input);

    CommandLineParser parser = new DefaultParser();
    HelpFormatter formatter = new HelpFormatter();
    CommandLine cmd;

    try {
        cmd = parser.parse(options, args);
    } catch (ParseException e) {
        System.out.println(e.getMessage());
        formatter.printHelp("fasttext.FastText", options);

        System.exit(1);
        return;
    }

    String inputModelPath = cmd.getOptionValue("input");

    logger.info("Loading fastText model to convert...");
    FastText model = FastText.loadModel(inputModelPath);
    FastTextPrediction label = model.predict("Good restaurant");
    System.out.println(label.label());
}
```

The output args are removed and we are giving a model as input and getting the parameters. Compile this and also copy the path to the FTZ model that we downloaded. We will test the library now:

```
$ mvn clean package
$ cp target/fasttext4j-0.2.1-SNAPSHOT.jar lib/fasttext4j-0.2.1-SNAPSHOT.jar
$ time bash fasttext-mmap.sh -i <path to>/dbpedia.ftz
__label__7
bash fasttext-mmap.sh -i 0.64s user 0.11s system 168% cpu 0.444 total
```

There will be a lot of logs as part of the output commands. We are not showing them here for now. Just check whether there are any error messages in the logs, which will probably mark the missing dependency libraries. Also, as you can see, loading and serving predictions from the FTZ file is quite fast on my local machine. The assumption is that it will be performant in a low-performing Android app as well.

Now that we have established that the library works and is able to give predictions, remove the `main` method as we won't be needing it in the Android app itself. Compile the JAR and place it in the `lib` folder:

```
$ mvn clean package
$ mvn install -Papp
$ unzip app/fasttext4j-app.zip
$ cp target/fasttext4j-0.2.1-SNAPSHOT.jar lib/fasttext4j-0.2.1-SNAPSHOT.jar
```

Adding the library dependencies to Android

Check in the `lib` folder. There will be placed all the libraries that are the dependencies for this project. We will need to add these dependencies to our Android application if we want to use this library.

Open **File** | **New** | **New Module...**:

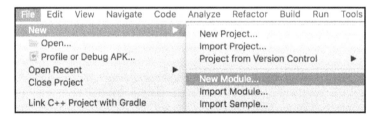

Import the JAR/AAR package:

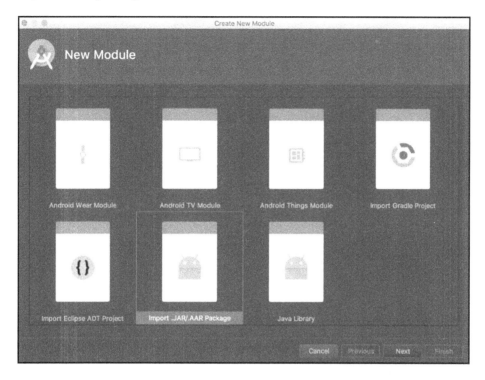

Now, add all the libraries in the `lib` folder to as dependencies. Now, your project structure should list the libraries as dependencies. Now, click on **app** | **dependencies** and add them as dependencies for the app as well. Add the library files as module dependencies:

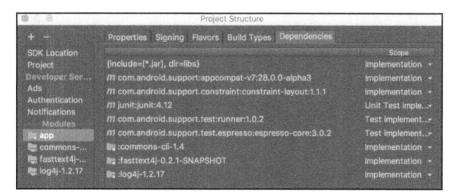

Now that the dependencies are there, we can start using the library in our activity.

Using library dependencies in Android

To use the library in Android, change `DisplayMessageActivity.java` and write the same code that you saw in the library testing phase.

Before compiling, add the `guava` dependency in your `gradle.build` file as the `UnsignedLong` dependencies in the `guava` library:

```
compile 'com.google.guava:guava:21.0'
```

Also, add the compile version so that it's able to compile the Java code:

```
apply plugin: 'com.android.application'

android {
    compileSdkVersion 28
    defaultConfig {
        ...
    }
    buildTypes {
        ...
    }
    compileOptions {
        sourceCompatibility JavaVersion.VERSION_1_8
        targetCompatibility JavaVersion.VERSION_1_8
    }
}

dependencies {
    ...
    compile 'com.google.guava:guava:21.0'
}
```

Finally the app

Now, compile the app and run it on your phone. You should be able to get the changes:

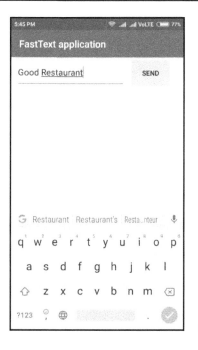 =>

Lets also take a look at the APK that was created. On my machine, the app size has changed to 4.6 MB. Small enough? I will leave it to you to be the judge of that:

```
$du -sh app-debug.apk
4.6M app-debug.apk
```

Summary

In this chapter, we took a look at the methodologies to implement fastText in a web and mobile context, focusing specifically on Android. We also took a look at the different considerations that you need to bear in mind, depending on whether you need to deploy on web or mobile. This should help you to create good applications and integrate fastText into your mobile applications.

Notes for the Readers

Windows and Linux

We would suggest that you use PowerShell for your windows command line as that is more powerful then simple `cmd`.

Task	Windows	Linux/macOS
Creating a directory	`mkdir`	`mkdir`
Change directory	`cd`	`cd`
Move files	`move`	`mv`
Unzip files	GUI and double click	`unzip`
Top of the file	`get-content`	`head`
Contents of the file	`type`	`cat`
Piping	`this pipes objects`	`this pipes text`
Bottom of the file	`-wait` parameter with `get-content`	`tail`

python and `perl` commands work the same way in windows as they work in bash and hence you can use those files and especially `perl` one liners in similar way.

Python 2 and Python 3

fastText works for both Python 2 and Python 3. There are few differences though that you should keep in mind for the particular python version.

1. `print` is a statement in Python 2 and a function in Python 3. This would mean that if you are in a Jupyter notebook and trying to see the changes in a variable you will need to pass the appropriate print statement in the corresponding python version.

2. The fastText handles text as Unicode. Python 3 also handles text as Unicode and hence there is no additional overhead if you code in Python 3. But in case you are developing your models in Python 2, you cannot have your data as a string instance. You will need to have your data as Unicode. Following is an example of text as an instance of the `str` class and `unicode` class in Python 2.

```
>>> text1 = "some text" # this will not work for fastText
>>> type(text1)
<type 'str'>
>>> text2 = unicode("some text") # in fastText you will need to use this.
>>> type(text2)
<type 'unicode'>
>>>
```

The fastText command line

Following is the list of parameters that you can use with fastText command line:

```
$ ./fasttext
usage: fasttext <command> <args>

The commands supported by fasttext are:

  supervised train a supervised classifier
  quantize quantize a model to reduce the memory usage
  test evaluate a supervised classifier
  predict predict most likely labels
  predict-prob predict most likely labels with probabilities
  skipgram train a skipgram model
  cbow train a cbow model
  print-word-vectors print word vectors given a trained model
  print-sentence-vectors print sentence vectors given a trained model
  print-ngrams print ngrams given a trained model and word
  nn query for nearest neighbors
```

```
analogies query for analogies
dump dump arguments,dictionary,input/output vectors
```

The supervised, skipgram, and cbow commands are for training a model. predict, predict-prob are for predictions on a supervised model. test, print-word-vectors, print-sentence-vectors, print-ngrams, nn, analogies can be used to evaluate the model. The dump command is basically to find the hyperparameters of the model and quantize is used to the compress the model.

The list of hyperparameters that you can use for training are listed later.

The fastText supervised

```
$ ./fasttext supervised
Empty input or output path.

The following arguments are mandatory:
  -input training file path
  -output output file path

The following arguments are optional:
  -verbose verbosity level [2]

The following arguments for the dictionary are optional:
  -minCount minimal number of word occurences [1]
  -minCountLabel minimal number of label occurences [0]
  -wordNgrams max length of word ngram [1]
  -bucket number of buckets [2000000]
  -minn min length of char ngram [0]
  -maxn max length of char ngram [0]
  -t sampling threshold [0.0001]
  -label labels prefix [__label__]

The following arguments for training are optional:
  -lr learning rate [0.1]
  -lrUpdateRate change the rate of updates for the learning rate [100]
  -dim size of word vectors [100]
  -ws size of the context window [5]
  -epoch number of epochs [5]
  -neg number of negatives sampled [5]
  -loss loss function {ns, hs, softmax} [softmax]
  -thread number of threads [12]
  -pretrainedVectors pretrained word vectors for supervised learning []
  -saveOutput whether output params should be saved [false]
```

The following arguments for quantization are optional:
  -cutoff number of words and ngrams to retain [0]
  -retrain whether embeddings are finetuned if a cutoff is applied [false]
  -qnorm whether the norm is quantized separately [false]
  -qout whether the classifier is quantized [false]
  -dsub size of each sub-vector [2]

The fastText skipgram

```
$ ./fasttext skipgram
Empty input or output path.

The following arguments are mandatory:
  -input training file path
  -output output file path

The following arguments are optional:
  -verbose verbosity level [2]

The following arguments for the dictionary are optional:
  -minCount minimal number of word occurences [5]
  -minCountLabel minimal number of label occurences [0]
  -wordNgrams max length of word ngram [1]
  -bucket number of buckets [2000000]
  -minn min length of char ngram [3]
  -maxn max length of char ngram [6]
  -t sampling threshold [0.0001]
  -label labels prefix [__label__]

The following arguments for training are optional:
  -lr learning rate [0.05]
  -lrUpdateRate change the rate of updates for the learning rate [100]
  -dim size of word vectors [100]
  -ws size of the context window [5]
  -epoch number of epochs [5]
  -neg number of negatives sampled [5]
  -loss loss function {ns, hs, softmax} [ns]
  -thread number of threads [12]
  -pretrainedVectors pretrained word vectors for supervised learning []
  -saveOutput whether output params should be saved [false]

The following arguments for quantization are optional:
  -cutoff number of words and ngrams to retain [0]
  -retrain whether embeddings are finetuned if a cutoff is applied [false]
  -qnorm whether the norm is quantized separately [false]
  -qout whether the classifier is quantized [false]
```

```
-dsub size of each sub-vector [2]
```

The fastText cbow

```
$ ./fasttext cbow
Empty input or output path.

The following arguments are mandatory:
 -input training file path
 -output output file path

The following arguments are optional:
 -verbose verbosity level [2]

The following arguments for the dictionary are optional:
 -minCount minimal number of word occurences [5]
 -minCountLabel minimal number of label occurences [0]
 -wordNgrams max length of word ngram [1]
 -bucket number of buckets [2000000]
 -minn min length of char ngram [3]
 -maxn max length of char ngram [6]
 -t sampling threshold [0.0001]
 -label labels prefix [__label__]

The following arguments for training are optional:
 -lr learning rate [0.05]
 -lrUpdateRate change the rate of updates for the learning rate [100]
 -dim size of word vectors [100]
 -ws size of the context window [5]
 -epoch number of epochs [5]
 -neg number of negatives sampled [5]
 -loss loss function {ns, hs, softmax} [ns]
 -thread number of threads [12]
 -pretrainedVectors pretrained word vectors for supervised learning []
 -saveOutput whether output params should be saved [false]

The following arguments for quantization are optional:
 -cutoff number of words and ngrams to retain [0]
 -retrain whether embeddings are finetuned if a cutoff is applied [false]
 -qnorm whether the norm is quantized separately [false]
 -qout whether the classifier is quantized [false]
 -dsub size of each sub-vector [2]
```

Gensim fastText parameters

Gensim supports the same hyperparameters that are supported in the native implementation of fastText. You should be able to set them as follows:

- `sentences`: This can be a list of list of tokens. In general, a stream of tokens is recommended, such as `LineSentence` from the word2vec module, as you have seen earlier. In the Facebook fastText library this is given by the path to the file and is given by the `-input` parameter.
- `sg`: Either 1 or 0. 1 means to train a skip-gram model, and 0 means to train a CBOW model. In the Facebook fastText library the equivalent is when you pass the `skipgram` and `cbow` arguments.
- `size`: The dimensions of the word vectors and hence must be an integer. In line with the original implementation, 100 is chosen as default. This is similar to the `-dim` argument in the Facebook fastText implementation.
- `window`: The window size that is considered around a word. This is the same as `-ws` argument in the original implementation.
- `alpha`: This is the initial learning rate and is a float. It is the same parameter as the `-lr` as what you saw in `Chapter 2`, *Creating Models Using FastText Command Line*.
- `min_alpha`: This is the min learning rate to which the learning rate will drop to as the training progresses.
- `seed`: This is for reproducability. For seeding to work the number of threads will also need to be 1.
- `min_count`: Minimum frequency of words in the documents below which the words will be discarded. Similar to the `-minCount` parameter in the command line.
- `max_vocab_size`: This is to limit the RAM size. In case there are more unique words than this will prune the less frequent ones. This needs to be decided based on top of the RAM that you have. For example, if you have 2 GB memory then `max_vocab_size` needs to be 10M * 2 = 20 million (20 000 000).
- `sample`: For down sampling of words. Similar to the "-t" parameter in fasttext command line.
- `workers`: Number of threads for training, similar to the `-thread` parameter in fastText command.

- `hs`: Either 0 or 1. If this is 1, then hierarchical softmax will be used as the loss function.
- `negative`: If you want to use negative sampling as the loss function, then set `hs=0` and negative to a non-zero positive number. Note that, there are only two functions that are supported for loss functions, hierarchical softmax and negative sampling. Simple softmax is not supported. This parameter, along with `hs` is the equivalent of the `-loss` parameter in the `fasttext` command.
- `cbow_mean`: There is a difference from the fastText command here. In the original implementation for `cbow` the mean of the vectors are taken. But in this case you have the option to use the sum by passing 0 and 1 in case you want to try out with the mean.
- `hashfxn`: Hash function for randomly initializing the weights.
- `iter`: Number of iterations or epochs over the samples. This is the same as the `-epoch` parameter in the command line.
- `trim_rule`: Function to specify if certain words should be kept in the vocabulary or trimmed away.
- `sorted_vocab`: Accepted values are 1 or 0. If 1 then the vocabulary will be sorted before indexing.
- `batch_words`: This is the target size of the batches that are passed. The default value is 10000. This is a bit similar to the `-lrUpdateRate` in the command line as the number of batches determine when the weights will be updated.
- `min_n` and `max_n`: Minimum and maximum length of the character n-grams.
- `word_ngrams`: Enriches subword information for use in the training process.
- bucket: The character n-grams are hashed on to a vector of fixed size. By default bucket size of 2 million words are used.
- `callbacks`: A list of callback functions to be executed at specific stages of the training process.

References

Chapter 3

- Word representations: `https://dl.acm.org/citation.cfm?id=1858721`
- One-hot encoding: `https://machinelearningmastery.com/how-to-one-hot-encode-sequence-data-in-python/`
- Representational learning: `https://github.com/anujgupta82/Representation-Learning-for-NLP`
- N-grams: `http://citeseerx.ist.psu.edu/viewdoc/summary?doi=10.1.1.53.9367`
- TF-IDF: `https://nlp.stanford.edu/IR-book/html/htmledition/inverse-document-frequency-1.html`
- Mikolov *et al*. 2013: `https://arxiv.org/abs/1310.4546`
- Maas and cgpotts paper: `https://web.stanford.edu/~cgpotts/papers/wvSent_acl2011.pdf`
- Bag of words in scikit-learn: `http://scikit-learn.org/stable/modules/feature_extraction.html#the-bag-of-words-representation`
- Kaggle word2vec `https://www.kaggle.com/c/word2vec-nlp-tutorial`
- Heap's law: `https://en.wikipedia.org/wiki/Heaps%27_law`
- Distributed representations of sentences and documents, Mikolov *et al*: `https://cs.stanford.edu/~quocle/paragraph_vector.pdf`
- CBOW: `https://towardsdatascience.com/understanding-feature-engineering-part-4-deep-learning-methods-for-text-data-96c44370bbfa`
- Skip-gram: McCormick, C. (2016, April 19), *Word2Vec Tutorial - The Skip-Gram Model* `http://mccormickml.com/2016/04/19/word2vec-tutorial-the-skip-gram-model/`
- TensorFlow implementation of word2vec: `https://github.com/tensorflow/tensorflow/blob/r1.1/tensorflow/examples/tutorials/word2vec/word2vec_basic.py`
- Word2vec explained: `https://arxiv.org/abs/1411.2738`
- Deriving negative sampling: `https://arxiv.org/abs/1402.3722`
- Compositional distributional semantics: `https://youtu.be/hTmKoHJw3Mg`

- The fastText and skipgram: `http://debajyotidatta.github.io/nlp/deep/learning/word-embeddings/2016/09/28/fast-text-and-skip-gram/`
- The skip-gram and CBOW: `https://iksinc.online/tag/continuous-bag-of-words-cbow/`
- Stanford lectures on CBOW and skip-gram: `https://cs224d.stanford.edu/lecture_notes/notes1.pdf`
- `http://mccormickml.com/assets/word2vec/Alex_Minnaar_Word2Vec_Tutorial_Part_II_The_Continuous_Bag-of-Words_Model.pdf`
- The fasttext PyTorch: `https://github.com/PetrochukM/PyTorch-NLP`
- Levy, Omer and Goldberg Yoav (2014), *Dependency-Based Word Embeddings*, 52nd Annual Meeting of the Association for Computational Linguistics, ACL 2014-Proceedings of the Conference, `2. 302-308. 10.3115/v1/P14-2050`
- *Notes on Noise Contrastive Estimation and Negative Sampling*: `https://arxiv.org/abs/1410.8251`
- *Sebastian Ruder, on word embeddings - Part 2: Approximating the Softmax*, `http://ruder.io/word-embeddings-softmax`, 2016.
- Scalable hierarchical distributed language model. `http://papers.nips.cc/paper/3583-a-scalable-hierarchical-distributed-language-model.pdf`
- Softmax function and its derivative. `https://eli.thegreenplace.net/2016/the-softmax-function-and-its-derivative/`
- *What is Softmax Regression and How is it Related to Logistic Regression?*, Sebastian Raschka. `https://www.kdnuggets.com/2016/07/softmax-regression-related-logistic-regression.html`
- `https://web.stanford.edu/class/cs224n/reports/2758157.pdf`
- Softmax regression, `http://ufldl.stanford.edu/tutorial/supervised/SoftmaxRegression/`
- Google Allo: `https://research.googleblog.com/2016/05/chat-smarter-with-allo.html`
- *Hierarchical Probabilistic Neural Network Language Model*, Morin and Bengio, 2005, `https://www.iro.umontreal.ca/~lisa/pointeurs/hierarchical-nnlm-aistats05.pdf`
- *A Scalable Hierarchical Distributed Language Model. Mnih, Andriy and Hinton, Geoffrey E. 2009*, `https://papers.nips.cc/paper/3583-a-scalable-hierarchical-distributed-language-model`
- *Self Organised Hierarchical Softmax*, `arXiv:1707.08588v1 [cs.CL] 26 Jul 2017`
- *Effective Text Clustering Method Based on Huffman Encoding Algorithm*, Nikhil Pawar, 2012, `https://www.ijsr.net/archive/v3i12/U1VCMTQ1NjE=.pdf`

- Tomas Mikolov, Ilya Sutskever, Kai Chen, Gregory S. Corrado, and Jeffrey Dean, *Distributed representations of words and phrases and their compositionality, In Advances in Neural Information Processing Systems 26: 27th Annual Conference on Neural Information Processing Systems 2013, Proceedings of a meeting held December 5-8, 2013, Lake Tahoe, Nevada, United States, pages 3111–3119, 2013.*

- http://debajyotidatta.github.io/nlp/deep/learning/word-embeddings/2016/09/28/fast-text-and-skip-gram/

- https://github.com/nzw0301/keras-examples/blob/master/Skip-gram-with-NS.ipynb

Chapter 4

- Vladimir Zolotov and David Kung 2017, *Analysis and Optimization of fastText Linear Text Classifier,* http://arxiv.org/abs/1702.05531

- *Text classification of linear models,* http://www.cs.umd.edu/class/fall2017/cmsc723/slides/slides_03.pdf

- *What is text classification,* Stanford, https://nlp.stanford.edu/IR-book/html/htmledition/the-text-classification-problem-1.html#sec:classificationproblem

- https://nlp.stanford.edu/IR-book/html/htmledition/text-classification-and-naive-bayes-1.html

- https://research.fb.com/fasttext/

- *Bag of tricks for efficient classification,* arXiv:1607.01759v3 [cs.CL] 9 Aug 2016

- https://github.com/poliglot/fasttext

- Joseph Turian, Lev Ratinov, and Yoshua Bengio, 2010, *Word representations: A simple and general method for semi-supervised learning, In Proceedings of the 48th Annual Meeting of the Association for Computational Linguistics (ACL '10), Association for Computational Linguistics, Stroudsburg, PA, USA, 384-394.*

- arXiv:1607.00570v1 [cs.IR] 2 Jul 2016

- *[Weinberger et al.2009] Kilian Weinberger, Anirban Dasgupta, John Langford, Alex Smola, and Josh Attenberg, 2009, Feature hashing for large scale multitask learning. In ICML*

- https://developers.googleblog.com/2018/04/text-embedding-models-contain-bias.html

- Softmax classifier in PyTorch: https://www.youtube.com/watch?v=lvNdl7yg4Pg

- *Hierarchical loss for classification*: arXiv:1709.01062v1 [cs.LG], 1 September 2017

- Svenstrup, Dan & Meinertz Hansen, Jonas & Winther, Ole. (2017), Hash Embeddings for Efficient Word Representations

- Explanation kernel trick, `https://www.quora.com/How-does-Kernel-compute-inner-product-in-higher-dimensional-space-without-visiting-that-space/answer/Jeremy-McMinis`

- `https://medium.com/value-stream-design/introducing-one-of-the-best-hacks-in-machine-learning-the-hashing-trick-bf6a9c8af18f`

- *Extremely Fast Text Feature Extraction for Classification and Indexing* by George Forman and Evan Kirshenbaum

- Armand Joulin, `et. al.` `FastText.zip`: *Compressing text classification model*, 2016, `https://arxiv.org/abs/1612.03651`

- Vector quantization, `https://www.slideshare.net/rajanisharmaa/vector-quantization`

- `http://shodhganga.inflibnet.ac.in/bitstream/10603/132782/14/12_chapter%204.pdf`

- *Voronoi Projection-Based Fast Nearest-Neighbor Search Algorithms: Box-Search and Mapping Table-Based Search Techniques, V. Ramasubramanian, K.K. Paliwa*l. 1997, `https://www.sciencedirect.com/science/article/pii/S1051200497903006`

- *How To Implement Learning Vector Quantization From Scratch With Python. Jason Brownie*, 2016, `https://machinelearningmastery.com/implement-learning-vector-quantization-scratch-python/`

- Herve Jegou, Matthijs Douze, and Cordelia Schmid, *Product quantization for nearest neighbor search*, IEEE Trans. PAMI, January 2011.

- Song Han, Huizi Mao, and William J Dally. Deep compression: *Compressing deep neural networks with pruning, trained quantization and huffman coding, In ICLR*, 2016

- Tiezheng Ge, Kaiming He, Qifa Ke, and Jian Sun, *Optimized product quantization for approximate nearest neighbor search. In CVPR*, June 2013

- *Expectation Maximisation*, Joydeep Bhattacharjee. `https://medium.com/technology-nineleaps/expectation-maximization-4bb203841757`

- Chen, Wenlin, Wilson, James T., Tyree, Stephen, Weinberger, Kilian Q, and Chen, Yixin, *Compressing neural networks with the hashing trick*, `arXiv:1504.04788`, `2015`

- Kai Zeng, Kun She, and Xinzheng Niu, *Feature Selection with Neighborhood Entropy-Based Cooperative Game Theory, Computational Intelligence and Neuroscience*, vol. 2014, Article ID 479289, 10 pages, 2014, `https://doi.org/10.1155/2014/479289`.

Chapter 5

- *Software Framework for Topic Modelling with Large Corpora*, Radim, 2010
- Gensim fastText Tutorial: `https://github.com/RaRe-Technologies/gensim/blob/develop/docs/notebooks/FastText_Tutorial.ipynb`
- P. Bojanowski, E. Grave, A. Joulin, T. Mikolov, *Enriching Word Vectors with Subword Information*, `https://arxiv.org/abs/1607.04606`
- `http://proceedings.mlr.press/v37/kusnerb15.pdf`
- Tomas Mikolov, Quoc V Le, Ilya Sutskever, 2013, (*Exploiting Similarities among Languages for Machine Translation*) (`https://arxiv.org/pdf/1309.4168.pdf`)
- Georgiana Dinu, Angelikie Lazaridou, and Marco Baroni. 2014, *Improving zero-shot learning by mitigating the hubness problem* (`https://arxiv.org/pdf/1412.6568.pdf`)
- The fastText normalization, `https://www.kaggle.com/mschumacher/using-fasttext-models-for-robust-embeddings/notebook`
- Luong, Minh-Thang and Socher, Richard and Manning, Christopher D. 2013, (*Better Word Representations with Recursive Neural Networks for Morphology*) (`https://nlp.stanford.edu/~lmthang/morphoNLM/`)

Chapter 6

- Yoav Goldberg (2015), *A Primer on Neural Network Models for Natural Language Processing*, (`https://arxiv.org/abs/1510.00726`)
- `http://www.wildml.com/2015/11/understanding-convolutional-neural-networksfor-nlp/`
- `http://mathworld.wolfram.com/Convolution.html`
- `http://www.joshuakim.io/understanding-how-convolutional-neural-network-cnn-perform-text-classification-with-word-embeddings/`
- `https://machinelearningmastery.com/best-practices-document-classification-deep-learning/`
- `https://keras.io/layers/embeddings/`
- `https://pytorch.org/tutorials/beginner/nlp/word_embeddings_tutorial.html`
- `https://pytorch.org/docs/master/nn.html`
- `https://stackoverflow.com/a/35688187`
- `http://www.brightideasinanalytics.com/rnn-pretrained-word-vectors/`

Chapter 7

- https://developer.android.com/training/basics/firstapp/
- https://github.com/sszuev/fastText_java
- https://stackoverflow.com/a/35369267
- https://developer.android.com/studio/publish/app-signing
- https://github.com/vinhkhuc/JFastText/blob/master/examples/api/src/main/java/ApiExample.java
- **The fastText issues:** https://github.com/vinhkhuc/JFastText/issues/28
- https://github.com/linkfluence/fastText4j/tree/master/src/main/java/fasttext

Other Books You May Enjoy

If you enjoyed this book, you may be interested in these other books by Packt:

Natural Language Processing with Python Cookbook
Krishna Bhavsar

ISBN: 9781787289321

- Explore corpus management using internal and external corpora
- Learn WordNet usage and a couple of simple application assignments using WordNet
- Operate on raw text
- Learn to perform tokenization, stemming, lemmatization, and spelling corrections, stop words removals, and more
- Understand regular expressions for pattern matching
- Learn to use and write your own POS taggers and grammars
- Learn to evaluate your own trained models
- Explore Deep Learning techniques in NLP
- Generate Text from Nietzsche's writing using LSTM
- Utilize the BABI dataset and LSTM to model episodes

Natural Language Processing with TensorFlow
Thushan Ganegedara

ISBN: 9781788478311

- Core concepts of NLP and various approaches to natural language processing
- How to solve NLP tasks by applying TensorFlow functions to create neural networks
- Strategies to process large amounts of data into word representations that can be used by deep learning applications
- Techniques for performing sentence classification and language generation using CNNs and RNNs
- About employing state-of-the art advanced RNNs, like long short-term memory, to solve complex text generation tasks
- How to write automatic translation programs and implement an actual neural machine translator from scratch
- The trends and innovations that are paving the future in NLP

Leave a review - let other readers know what you think

Please share your thoughts on this book with others by leaving a review on the site that you bought it from. If you purchased the book from Amazon, please leave us an honest review on this book's Amazon page. This is vital so that other potential readers can see and use your unbiased opinion to make purchasing decisions, we can understand what our customers think about our products, and our authors can see your feedback on the title that they have worked with Packt to create. It will only take a few minutes of your time, but is valuable to other potential customers, our authors, and Packt. Thank you!

Index

www.ingramcontent.com/pod-product-compliance
Lightning Source LLC
Chambersburg PA
CBHW080528060326
40690CB00022B/5069